GARDEN *of* GRAPES.

First Edition: 2023

Published by Garden of Grapes.

Printed in USA

Library of Congress Cataloging-in-Publication Data:

First edition.
Includes index.

Manufactured in USA

Introduction

Ladies and gentlemen, home cooks and culinary adventurers,

Welcome to "Weeknight Wonders: A 5-Ingredient Cookbook." I'm thrilled to take you on this gastronomic journey, a journey that redefines the way we think about weeknight dinners. In a world where time is a precious commodity, this cookbook is a testament to the fact that creating delicious, satisfying meals doesn't require an extensive list of ingredients or hours spent in the kitchen.

So, why this cookbook, and what can you expect from it?

The inspiration for this culinary endeavor is born from a very relatable and universal experience: the weeknight hustle. We've all been there, haven't we? After a long day at work or a whirlwind of errands, the last thing you want is to wrestle with a complex recipe that demands a pantry full of exotic ingredients and hours of cooking. This cookbook is a response to that everyday challenge. It's an answer to the question: "What can I put on the table tonight that's not only easy but absolutely delicious?"

In "Weeknight Wonders," we're focusing on the magical number five. Five ingredients are all you need to whip up extraordinary dishes. With just a handful of elements, carefully selected for their flavor and impact, we'll transform your weeknight dinners into something you anticipate, savor, and cherish.

This cookbook isn't just about simplicity; it's about maximizing flavor. It's about those few key ingredients that can make a meal memorable. It's about the pleasure of tasting the essence of each element as it combines to create a harmonious, satisfying whole. It's about putting a chef's secret weapon into the hands of home cooks, without the fuss or the fanfare.

As we journey through these pages, you'll discover a treasure trove of recipes that make every night a weeknight wonder. From succulent mains to delightful sides and tempting desserts, each dish has been meticulously crafted with the busy home chef in mind. There's something for every palate and every occasion, ensuring that your dinner table is never short of a delightful surprise.

I'm confident you'll be amazed at the fantastic results you can achieve with just a few ingredients, a bit of culinary imagination, and the guidance provided within these pages. Whether you're an experienced cook or just starting your culinary adventure, these recipes are designed to make you feel like a seasoned chef every night of the week.

So, get ready to embark on a culinary journey that will redefine the way you think about weeknight dinners. "Weeknight Wonders" is more than a cookbook; it's an invitation to explore the magic of simple, flavorful cooking. It's a reminder that amidst the chaos of our daily lives, the joy of a remarkable meal is always within reach.

Thank you for being part of this journey. Let's make every weeknight a wonder, one delicious dish at a time.

With pots and pans at the ready,

Butternut Squash Salad
See page, 19

Cooking Philosophy or Approach

Ladies and gentlemen, food lovers, and culinary enthusiasts,

As we delve into the heart and soul of "Weeknight Wonders: A 5-Ingredient Cookbook," it's only fitting to explore the underlying philosophy that has driven the creation of these delectable recipes.

Cooking, as I've come to know it over countless stints in professional kitchens and countless moments of sheer delight in the company of a well-prepared meal, is a journey of both simplicity and passion. It's about taking the most basic of ingredients and crafting them into something extraordinary. That's the essence of this cookbook.

The guiding principle behind "Weeknight Wonders" is to make the joy of cooking accessible to everyone, especially during those hustle-and-bustle weeknights when time is a luxury. Our approach hinges on two fundamental tenets: quality and simplicity.

Quality, as any discerning cook knows, starts with the ingredients. While we're focusing on recipes with just five key components, the quality of each is paramount. Freshness, flavor, and the integrity of each ingredient play a starring role in ensuring that the end result is nothing short of amazing. I've always believed that when you use top-notch ingredients, the flavors speak for themselves.

Simplicity, the second pillar of our culinary philosophy, is the beacon that guides these recipes. We understand that not every meal needs to be a laborious endeavor or require a multitude of pots, pans, and ingredients. With the right approach, you can whip up a culinary masterpiece in a fraction of the time. It's about embracing the elegance of minimalism while maximizing the taste.

The magic happens when you combine these principles – quality and simplicity. It's about respecting the ingredients, letting them shine in their own right, and orchestrating them into harmonious, delicious creations. In these pages, you'll find techniques that bring out the best in each component, allowing their natural flavors to meld and elevate the dish to a level of satisfaction that's hard to match.

Though we're working with only five ingredients per recipe, the culinary world is vast, and so are the possibilities. You'll find dishes that span the globe, from the heartwarming comfort of Italian pasta to the bold flavors of Mexican cuisine. The techniques you'll encounter are tried and true, designed to coax the most flavor from every ingredient without overwhelming you with complex steps.

So, whether you're a seasoned chef looking for some weeknight inspiration or a novice just starting your culinary adventure, you're in the right place. "Weeknight Wonders" is your passport to creating gourmet experiences right in your own kitchen, with ease and grace.

Here's to embracing the simplicity and quality that fine cooking embodies, one delicious, five-ingredient meal at a time. May your weeknights be filled with the wonders of good food, great company, and the joy of cooking.

With a pinch of salt, a dash of inspiration, and a world of flavor,

Lemon Garlic Roast Chicken
See page, 24

Tips for Successful Cooking

Ladies and gentlemen, home cooks and culinary adventurers,

In the pages of "Weeknight Wonders: A 5-Ingredient Cookbook," we've embarked on a mission to make your weeknight dinners not only hassle-free but truly delightful. You've explored a world of flavors and dishes that can be conjured with just a handful of ingredients. You're well on your way to becoming a weeknight wizard, a maestro of quick and easy culinary wonders.

But what's the secret to turning this collection of recipes into weeknight magic? The answer lies in mastering a few key cooking tips and techniques. So, as you set forth on your gastronomic journey, let's arm you with some sage advice to ensure your culinary success.

1. Organization is Your Sous-Chef: Before you even touch a pan or pot, read through your chosen recipe. Ensure you have all the ingredients at your fingertips, measured and prepped. This is the culinary equivalent of a battle plan. A well-organized kitchen sets the stage for triumph.

2. The Right Tools: Just as a painter needs brushes and a musician needs instruments, a chef needs the right tools. Equip your kitchen with essential items like sharp knives, a sturdy cutting board, quality cookware, and reliable kitchen gadgets. The right tools are your allies in the kitchen.

3. Quality over Quantity: When it comes to ingredients, especially in recipes that rely on just a handful, quality reigns supreme. Opt for the freshest produce, the finest cuts of meat, and the best spices you can get your hands on. Great ingredients elevate a dish from good to unforgettable.

4. Respect the Order: Every recipe has a sequence, a particular order in which ingredients are added and techniques employed. Follow this order diligently. It's the roadmap to success. Respect the process, and your dish will turn out just as planned.

5. The Power of Seasoning: Seasoning isn't just about adding salt and pepper. It's about balancing flavors. Taste as you go and adjust the seasoning as needed. Don't be afraid to explore with herbs, spices, and seasonings that complement the dish.

6. Don't Rush the Sear: When a recipe calls for searing meat, give it the time it deserves. That golden crust is flavor in the making. Rushing this step can result in a pale imitation of the dish's full potential.

7. Rest for the Best: Before diving into your creation, let it rest for a few minutes. This allows flavors to meld, juices to redistribute, and your dish to reach its peak.

8. Patience is a Virtue: Not every recipe will come together in five minutes, and that's perfectly okay. Good food is worth waiting for. Your patience will be rewarded with a marvelous meal.

9. Trial and Error: Cooking is an art, not an exact science. Don't be disheartened by minor mishaps. Sometimes, the best dishes are born from a creative twist or a simple mistake. Embrace the adventure and trust your instincts.

In "Weeknight Wonders," you have the tools, the ingredients, and the inspiration. Now, armed with these tips, you have the wisdom. It's time to turn your weeknights into culinary celebrations. Remember, the most essential ingredient is your love for cooking. So, put on your apron, unleash your inner chef, and let the magic unfold in your kitchen.

Here's to countless more weeknight wonders and to the joy of creating memorable meals with just five ingredients.

Honey Mustard Glazed Salmon
See page, 27

Kitchen Essentials

Ladies and gentlemen, home cooks and culinary adventurers,

In the realm of cooking, the heart of your culinary journey isn't just the ingredients; it's the tools you employ to transform them into delectable dishes. Here in "Weeknight Wonders: A 5-Ingredient Cookbook," our kitchen essentials are simple yet pivotal, a collection of trusty sidekicks that will stand by you on your quest to create quick, satisfying weeknight meals.

1. The Chef's Knife: Ah, the chef's knife, a kitchen classic that's your trusty companion in virtually every culinary escapade. Its sharp blade is your path to precision, from dicing onions to slicing juicy tomatoes. Make sure it's always sharp, and it will reward you with efficiency and elegance in your preparations.

2. Cutting Boards: The faithful stage for your ingredient prepping, cutting boards come in various materials, from wood to plastic. They are essential for maintaining your knife's edge and keeping your countertops intact.

3. Measuring Cups and Spoons: Precision in cooking is often the difference between success and an almost-there dish. These instruments ensure that you add just the right amount of that secret sauce, be it flour, sugar, or a splash of olive oil.

4. Non-Stick Skillet: A non-stick skillet is your secret weapon for fuss-free cooking. From sautéing vegetables to searing meats, it's the go-to pan for delicious meals without the drama of sticky, stubborn food clinging to the surface.

5. Spatula: The spatula is your trusty kitchen sidekick, whether you're flipping pancakes, gently stirring ingredients, or coaxing that perfect omelet from the pan. Look for a heat-resistant, versatile spatula that can take the heat and keep your meals intact.

6. Pot and Pan Set: A good quality pot and pan set is indispensable for simmering, boiling, and braising. It's the vessel of creation for soups, sauces, and pasta, and it's where your culinary magic often begins.

7. Ovenware: For dishes that require a little oven love, having a set of oven-safe dishes and bakeware is essential. From casseroles to roasting vegetables, this is where the flavors mingle and intensify.

8. Grater: The grater is the tool that unveils the hidden secrets of ingredients like cheese, zesty citrus, and aromatic spices. It's your key to infusing that extra layer of flavor and texture into your dishes.

Now that you've met our indispensable kitchen tools, let's talk about how to wield them with precision and finesse:

- Knife Skills: Respect the blade. Learn proper knife skills for efficient, safe, and elegant cutting.

- Measuring Matters: Precision in measurements is the cornerstone of cooking, especially in baking. For liquids, use a clear liquid measuring cup, and for dry ingredients, fill your measuring cup and level it off with a knife.

- Non-Stick Mastery: When using a non-stick skillet, moderate heat is your ally. High heat can damage the non-stick coating, so keep it at a medium or lower setting.

- Pan Patience: Give your pans time to heat up. A preheated pan ensures that your food sears rather than steams.

- One-Pot Magic: Embrace the elegance of one-pot cooking. Many of our recipes in this cookbook are designed for simplicity, and the magic happens all in one pot.

We hope these essential tools and tips help you on your journey through "Weeknight Wonders." With these instruments at your side and the knowledge of how to wield them, you're ready to conquer the culinary challenges that weeknight dinners may throw your way.

Cook with confidence, and may your kitchen be filled with the enchanting aromas of success and satisfaction.

Happy cooking!

Flavor Pairing Suggestions

Dear Culinary Explorers,

As you've journeyed through the pages of "Weeknight Wonders: A 5-Ingredient Cookbook," you've already experienced the magic of creating exquisite dishes with just a handful of elements. You've tasted the simplicity and elegance of these recipes, but I'm here to help you take your culinary adventure to the next level.

Cooking, at its heart, is an art of balance, contrast, and harmony. It's a symphony of flavors, a dance of ingredients that come together to create a perfect bite. To truly master this culinary craft, you must understand how different flavors and ingredients play off one another, how they amplify or soften each other's characteristics, and how they come together to tantalize your taste buds.

To aid you on this journey of flavor exploration and experimentation, I'd like to offer some flavor pairing suggestions. These are more than just combinations of ingredients; they're invitations to a world of creativity and invention in your own kitchen. Use them as a springboard to create your unique recipes, or let them inspire you to enhance the dishes you've already come to love within this cookbook.

1. Tangy Citrus & Sweet Honey: The bright, zesty notes of citrus, whether from lemons, oranges, or limes, can be beautifully balanced with the richness of honey. Drizzle citrus-infused honey over your dishes for a burst of refreshing sweetness.

2. Earthy Mushrooms & Fresh Herbs: Earthy mushrooms find harmony with the freshness of herbs like rosemary, thyme, and sage. Add these herbs to your mushroom-based dishes to elevate their depth of flavor.

3. Spicy Chili & Cooling Yogurt: When you're creating a spicy masterpiece, the cool creaminess of yogurt provides the perfect counterpoint. Drizzle yogurt-based sauces over your spicy dishes to soothe the heat.

4. Salty Bacon & Sweet Maple: The marriage of salty and sweet is a timeless favorite. Complement your bacon-infused creations with a drizzle of maple syrup for an unforgettable flavor experience.

5. Roasted Nuts & Savory Herbs: Roasted nuts, like almonds or walnuts, pair beautifully with savory herbs such as thyme, rosemary, or oregano. Toss these herbed nuts into your dishes for a delightful crunch and aromatic depth.

6. Creamy Avocado & Bright Cilantro: The rich creaminess of avocado is balanced perfectly with the bright, citrusy notes of cilantro. Combine these two ingredients in your recipes for a burst of freshness.

7. Rich Chocolate & Floral Vanilla: For those indulgent moments, the combination of rich, dark chocolate with the floral hints of vanilla is a match made in heaven. Let this duo enhance your dessert creations.

8. Savory Parmesan & Pungent Garlic: The umami-rich parmesan cheese becomes even more robust with the addition of pungent garlic. Add minced or roasted garlic to your parmesan-infused dishes for a flavorful punch.

These are just a few suggestions to ignite your culinary imagination. Use these ideas as stepping stones, but don't be afraid to wander off the beaten path. Experiment, create, and surprise your taste buds with your culinary discoveries. After all, cooking is about more than just following recipes; it's about making them your own.

The culinary world is your canvas, and the ingredients are your palette. With "Weeknight Wonders" as your guide, you're well on your way to becoming a kitchen artist. So, don your apron, grab your utensils, and let your taste buds be your muse.

Happy cooking and, as always, may your kitchen be filled with love, laughter, and unforgettable flavors.

Table of contents

Chapter 1:
Speedy Starters

4
skewers

150

15 mins

Caprese Skewers

A Mediterranean classic, these skewers burst with the flavors of Italy. Fresh mozzarella, cherry tomatoes, and basil leaves come together in perfect harmony.

Ingredients:

- 12 cherry tomatoes
- 12 fresh mozzarella balls
- 12 basil leaves
- 2 tbsp extra-virgin olive oil
- 2 tbsp balsamic glaze
- Salt and pepper to taste

Directions

1. Thread a tomato, mozzarella ball, and basil leaf onto each skewer.
2. Drizzle with olive oil and balsamic glaze.
3. Season with salt and pepper.
4. Serve immediately.

Fun Facts

Did you know? The name "Caprese" comes from the island of Capri, where this salad was created.

12 dates | 180 | 20 mins

Bacon-Wrapped Dates

Ingredients:

- 12 large Medjool dates
- 4 oz goat cheese
- 6 slices bacon, cut in half widthwise

Sweet meets savory in this irresistible appetizer. Dates stuffed with creamy goat cheese and wrapped in smoky bacon.

Directions

1. Preheat oven to 375°F (190°C).
2. Slice each date lengthwise, remove the pit.
3. Fill each date with goat cheese.
4. Wrap with half a bacon slice.
5. Secure with toothpicks.
6. Bake for 15-20 mins, until bacon is crisp.
7. Serve warm.

Fun Facts

Fun Fact: Bacon-wrapped dates are known as "Devils on Horseback" in British cuisine.

8
servings

120

25 mins

Creamy Spinach Dip

Ingredients:

- 8 oz cream cheese
- 1 cup sour cream
- 1 cup chopped spinach (frozen, thawed, and drained)
- 1/2 cup grated Parmesan cheese
- 1/4 cup mayonnaise
- 1 tsp garlic powder
- Salt and pepper to taste

Dive into a bowl of creamy goodness with this spinach dip. Perfect for dipping bread, chips, or veggies.

Directions

1. In a bowl, mix cream cheese, sour cream, spinach, Parmesan, mayonnaise, and garlic powder.
2. Season with salt and pepper.
3. Chill for 1 hour before serving.
4. Enjoy with your favorite dippers!

Fun Facts

Spinach dip was originally created as a marketing tool by Knorr in the 1950s.

12 sticks   220   30 mins

Garlic Parmesan Breadsticks

Ingredients:

- 1 lb pizza dough
- 1/4 cup unsalted butter (melted)
- 2 cloves garlic (minced)
- 1/4 cup grated Parmesan cheese
- 1/4 cup chopped fresh parsley

These breadsticks are the perfect combination of crispy and cheesy, with a hint of garlic. Guaranteed crowd-pleasers.

Directions

1. Preheat oven to 375°F (190°C).
2. Roll out pizza dough into a rectangle.
3. Cut into 12 strips.
4. Combine melted butter and garlic.
5. Brush over dough strips.
6. Sprinkle with Parmesan and parsley.
7. Bake for 15-20 mins until golden.
8. Serve warm.

Fun Facts

Fun Fact: Breadsticks have been a part of Italian cuisine since ancient Rome.

12 mushrooms

70

30 mins

Stuffed Mushrooms with Herbs

Ingredients:

- 12 large mushrooms
- 1/2 cup breadcrumbs
- 1/4 cup grated Parmesan cheese
- 2 cloves garlic (minced)
- 2 tbsp fresh parsley (chopped)
- 2 tbsp olive oil
- Salt and pepper to taste

These mushrooms are a flavor explosion. Filled with a savory mixture of herbs, breadcrumbs, and Parmesan cheese.

Directions

1. Preheat oven to 375°F (190°C).
2. Remove mushroom stems and chop them.
3. Mix chopped stems with breadcrumbs, Parmesan, garlic, and parsley.
4. Stuff mushroom caps with the mixture.
5. Drizzle with olive oil.
6. Bake for 20-25 mins.
7. Serve hot.

Fun Facts

Did you know? Mushrooms are a good source of umami, the fifth taste sensation.

6 servings

90

15 mins

Avocado Salsa

Ingredients:

- 2 ripe avocados (diced)
- 1 cup diced tomatoes
- 1/2 cup diced red onion
- 1/4 cup chopped cilantro
- 2 cloves garlic (minced)
- 1 jalapeño (seeded and minced)
- Juice of 2 limes
- Salt and pepper to taste

Fresh, creamy, and full of zesty flavors, this avocado salsa is perfect for scooping with tortilla chips.

Directions

1. In a bowl, combine avocados, tomatoes, red onion, cilantro, garlic, and jalapeño.
2. Squeeze lime juice over the mixture.
3. Season with salt and pepper.
4. Serve chilled.

Fun Facts

Fun Fact: Avocado is a fruit, not a vegetable, and it's sometimes called "alligator pear" due to its shape and rough skin.

4
servings

160

10 mins

Pita Chips with Hummus

Ingredients:

- 4 pita bread rounds
- 2 tbsp olive oil
- 1 tsp paprika
- 1/2 tsp garlic powder
- Salt to taste
- 1 cup hummus (store-bought or homemade)

Crispy pita chips paired with creamy hummus – a classic Middle Eastern combination that never goes out of style.

Directions

1. Preheat oven to 375°F (190°C).
2. Cut pita bread into wedges.
3. In a bowl, mix olive oil, paprika, garlic powder, and salt.
4. Toss pita wedges in the mixture.
5. Arrange on a baking sheet and bake for 8-10 mins.
6. Serve with hummus.

Fun Facts

Did you know? Hummus has been consumed for over a thousand years, with its origins traced back to ancient Egypt.

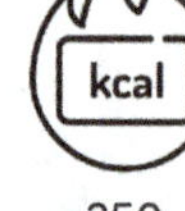

12
sandwic
hes

250

20 mins

Mini BLT Sandwiches

Ingredients:

- 24 small slices of bread (white or whole wheat)
- 12 slices bacon (cooked and cut in half)
- 12 cherry tomatoes (sliced)
- 1 cup lettuce (shredded)
- 1/2 cup mayonnaise
- Salt and pepper to taste

These mini BLTs are a bite-sized delight. Crispy bacon, fresh lettuce, and juicy tomatoes, all nestled between tiny slices of bread.

Directions

1. Spread mayonnaise on each slice of bread.
2. Top half of the slices with bacon, tomatoes, and lettuce.
3. Season with salt and pepper.
4. Place the remaining bread slices on top to make sandwiches.
5. Serve as appetizers or snacks.

Fun Facts

BLT stands for "Bacon, Lettuce, and Tomato," and it's believed to have originated in the early 20th century.

4
servings

120

35 mins

Spicy Buffalo Cauliflower Bites

Ingredients:

- 1 small cauliflower head (cut into florets)
- 1/2 cup flour
- 1/2 cup water
- 1 tsp garlic powder
- 1 tsp paprika
- 1/2 cup buffalo sauce
- 2 tbsp butter (melted)
- Ranch or blue cheese dressing (for dipping)

A healthier take on classic buffalo wings. These cauliflower bites are baked to crispy perfection and smothered in spicy sauce.

Directions

1. Preheat oven to 450°F (230°C).
2. In a bowl, whisk flour, water, garlic powder, and paprika to make a batter.
3. Dip cauliflower florets in the batter and place on a baking sheet.
4. Bake for 20-25 mins until crispy.
5. In a separate bowl, mix buffalo sauce and melted butter.
6. Toss cauliflower in the sauce.
7. Serve with dressing.

Fun Facts

Cauliflower is a versatile vegetable that can mimic the texture of meat when cooked, making it a popular choice for vegetarian and vegan dishes.

6
servings

130

15 mins

Tomato Basil Bruschetta

Ingredients:

- 4 ripe tomatoes (diced)
- 1/4 cup fresh basil (chopped)
- 2 cloves garlic (minced)
- 2 tbsp extra-virgin olive oil
- 1 tsp balsamic vinegar
- Salt and pepper to taste
- 1 baguette (sliced)

This classic Italian appetizer is a symphony of fresh tomatoes, basil, and garlic, served on crispy slices of toasted baguette.

Directions

1. In a bowl, combine tomatoes, basil, garlic, olive oil, and balsamic vinegar.
2. Season with salt and pepper.
3. Toast baguette slices until golden.
4. Spoon the tomato mixture onto the slices.
5. Serve immediately.

Fun Facts

Fun Fact: Bruschetta originated in ancient Rome, where olive oil and garlic were used to season stale bread.

Chapter 2:
Soups & Salads in a Snap

4
servings

180

30 mins

Tomato Basil Soup

Ingredients:

- 6 ripe tomatoes (chopped)
- 1/2 cup fresh basil leaves (chopped)
- 1 onion (chopped)
- 2 cloves garlic (minced)
- 2 cups vegetable broth
- 1/2 cup heavy cream
- Salt and pepper to taste

A comforting classic, this tomato basil soup is like a warm hug in a bowl. Made with ripe tomatoes, fresh basil, and a hint of cream.

Directions

1. In a pot, sauté onion and garlic until soft.
2. Add tomatoes and basil, cook for 5 mins.
3. Pour in vegetable broth and simmer for 20 mins.
4. Blend until smooth.
5. Stir in heavy cream, season with salt and pepper.
6. Serve hot.

Fun Facts

Did you know? Tomato soup has been a popular dish in America since the late 19th century.

6 servings

250

40 mins

Chicken Noodle Soup

Ingredients:

- 2 boneless, skinless chicken breasts
- 6 cups chicken broth
- 2 carrots (sliced)
- 2 celery stalks (sliced)
- 1 onion (chopped)
- 2 cloves garlic (minced)
- 1 cup egg noodles
- Salt and pepper to taste

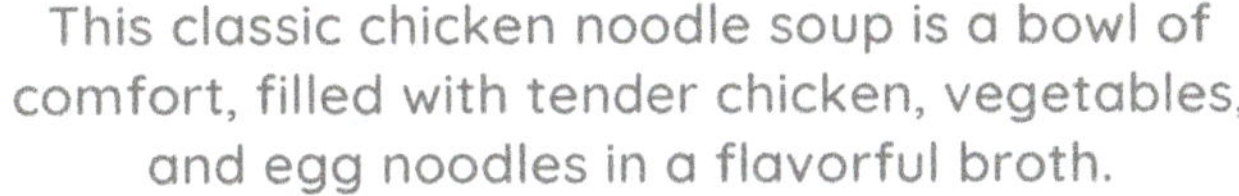

This classic chicken noodle soup is a bowl of comfort, filled with tender chicken, vegetables, and egg noodles in a flavorful broth.

Directions

1. In a large pot, bring chicken broth to a boil.
2. Add chicken breasts, carrots, celery, onion, and garlic.
3. Simmer for 20 mins until chicken is cooked.
4. Remove chicken, shred it, and return to the pot.
5. Add egg noodles and cook until tender.
6. Season with salt and pepper.
7. Serve hot.

Fun Facts

Chicken noodle soup is believed to have originated in ancient China over 2,000 years ago.

4
servings

180

15 mins

Greek Salad

Ingredients:

- 2 cucumbers (sliced)
- 4 tomatoes (chopped)
- 1 red onion (sliced)
- 1/2 cup Kalamata olives
- 1/2 cup crumbled feta cheese
- 2 tbsp olive oil
- 1 tsp dried oregano
- Salt and pepper to taste

Transport yourself to Greece with this refreshing salad. Crisp cucumbers, juicy tomatoes, Kalamata olives, and feta cheese with a tangy dressing.

Directions

1. In a large bowl, combine cucumbers, tomatoes, red onion, olives, and feta cheese.
2. Drizzle with olive oil.
3. Sprinkle with oregano, salt, and pepper.
4. Toss gently to coat.
5. Serve chilled.

Fun Facts

Fun Fact: Greek salad is also known as "Horiatiki," which means "village salad" in Greek.

4
servings

250

20 mins

Caesar Salad

Ingredients:

- 1 head romaine lettuce (torn into bite-sized pieces)
- 1 cup croutons
- 1/2 cup grated Parmesan cheese
- 1/2 cup Caesar dressing
- Salt and pepper to taste

Crisp romaine lettuce, garlicky croutons, and Parmesan cheese come together in this iconic salad. Tossed in a creamy Caesar dressing.

Directions

1. In a large bowl, combine romaine lettuce, croutons, and Parmesan cheese.
2. Drizzle with Caesar dressing.
3. Season with salt and pepper.
4. Toss until well coated.
5. Serve immediately.

Fun Facts

Did you know? Caesar salad was invented in Tijuana, Mexico, by Caesar Cardini in the 1920s.

4
servings

150

15 mins

Spinach and Strawberry Salad

Ingredients:

- 6 cups fresh spinach
- 1 cup strawberries (sliced)
- 1/4 cup sliced almonds (toasted)
- 1/4 cup balsamic vinaigrette dressing
- Salt and pepper to taste

A delightful combination of fresh spinach, sweet strawberries, toasted almonds, and a tangy vinaigrette.

Directions

1. In a bowl, combine spinach, strawberries, and toasted almonds.
2. Drizzle with balsamic vinaigrette dressing.
3. Season with salt and pepper.
4. Toss gently.
5. Serve immediately.

Fun Facts

Fun Fact: Spinach is known for its high iron content, but it's also a good source of vitamins and antioxidants.

4
servings

220

35 mins

Creamy Tomato Bisque

A velvety smooth tomato bisque with a touch of creaminess. Perfect for a cozy evening.

Ingredients:

- 2 cans (28 oz each) crushed tomatoes
- 1 cup heavy cream
- 1/2 cup vegetable broth
- 1 onion (chopped)
- 2 cloves garlic (minced)
- 2 tbsp butter
- 1 tsp sugar
- Salt and pepper to taste

Directions

1. In a pot, melt butter and sauté onion and garlic until soft.
2. Add crushed tomatoes, sugar, and vegetable broth.
3. Simmer for 20 mins.
4. Blend until smooth.
5. Return to the pot, stir in heavy cream.
6. Season with salt and pepper.
7. Heat gently, then serve.

Fun Facts

Tomato bisque is often served as a starter in fine dining restaurants due to its smooth and elegant texture.

4 servings

200

30 mins

Butternut Squash Salad

Roasted butternut squash, mixed greens, cranberries, and a maple vinaigrette create a salad that's both hearty and sweet.

Ingredients:

- 4 cups butternut squash (cubed)
- 6 cups mixed greens
- 1/2 cup dried cranberries
- 1/4 cup chopped pecans (toasted)
- 2 tbsp maple vinaigrette dressing
- Salt and pepper to taste

Directions

1. Toss butternut squash with olive oil, salt, and pepper.
2. Roast at 400°F (200°C) for 20-25 mins until tender.
3. In a bowl, combine mixed greens, cranberries, and pecans.
4. Drizzle with maple vinaigrette dressing.
5. Add roasted squash on top.
6. Serve warm or chilled.

Fun Facts

Butternut squash is rich in vitamins A and C, as well as fiber, making it a nutritious addition to your salad.

6
servings

180

40 mins

Lentil Soup

Hearty and wholesome, this lentil soup is packed with protein and flavor. A perfect bowl of comfort on a chilly day.

Ingredients:

- 1 cup dried green or brown lentils
- 1 onion (chopped)
- 2 carrots (chopped)
- 2 celery stalks (chopped)
- 2 cloves garlic (minced)
- 6 cups vegetable broth
- 1 tsp cumin
- Salt and pepper to taste

Directions

1. In a pot, sauté onion, garlic, carrots, and celery until softened.
2. Add lentils, vegetable broth, and cumin.
3. Simmer for 30 mins until lentils are tender.
4. Season with salt and pepper.
5. Serve hot.

Fun Facts

Lentils are one of the oldest cultivated crops and have been eaten for over 13,000 years.

6
servings

280

25 mins

Caesar Pasta Salad

Ingredients:

- 8 oz bowtie pasta (cooked and cooled)
- 2 cups cooked chicken (shredded)
- 1 cup cherry tomatoes (halved)
- 1/2 cup grated Parmesan cheese
- 1/2 cup Caesar dressing
- Salt and pepper to taste

A twist on the classic Caesar, this pasta salad features bowtie pasta, chicken, cherry tomatoes, and a creamy Caesar dressing.

Directions

1. In a large bowl, combine pasta, chicken, cherry tomatoes, and Parmesan cheese.
2. Drizzle with Caesar dressing.
3. Season with salt and pepper.
4. Toss until well coated.
5. Serve chilled.

Fun Facts

Pasta salad variations are popular at picnics and potlucks due to their versatility and ability to feed a crowd.

4
servings

80

15 mins

Cucumber and Dill Salad

This light and refreshing salad is a perfect side dish. Crisp cucumbers, tangy yogurt, and fresh dill create a harmonious medley.

Ingredients:

- 2 cucumbers (sliced)
- 1/2 cup Greek yogurt
- 2 tbsp fresh dill (chopped)
- 1 tbsp lemon juice
- Salt and pepper to taste

Directions

1. In a bowl, combine sliced cucumbers and Greek yogurt.
2. Add fresh dill and lemon juice.
3. Season with salt and pepper.
4. Toss gently to coat.
5. Serve chilled.

Fun Facts

Cucumber and dill salad is a common side dish in many Eastern European cuisines, including Russian and Ukrainian.

Chapter 3:
Marvelous Meat Dishes

4 servings

300

40 mins

Lemon Garlic Roast Chicken

Ingredients:

- 1 whole chicken (about 4 lbs)
- 4 cloves garlic (minced)
- Zest and juice of 2 lemons
- 2 tbsp olive oil
- 1 tbsp fresh rosemary (chopped)
- Salt and pepper to taste

This roast chicken is a burst of flavor with zesty lemon and aromatic garlic. Juicy and tender, it's a family favorite.

Directions

1. Preheat oven to 375°F (190°C).
2. In a bowl, mix garlic, lemon zest, lemon juice, olive oil, rosemary, salt, and pepper.
3. Rub the mixture over the chicken.
4. Roast in the oven for 1 hour or until the internal temperature reaches 165°F (74°C).
5. Let it rest for 10 mins before carving.
6. Serve with pan juices.

Fun Facts

Roast chicken is a classic comfort food that has been enjoyed for centuries in various cultures.

6
sandwic
hes

350

8 hours

BBQ Pulled Pork Sandwiches

Ingredients:

- 3 lbs pork shoulder or butt roast
- 1 cup barbecue sauce
- 1/2 cup apple cider vinegar
- 1/4 cup brown sugar
- 1 tsp smoked paprika
- 1/2 tsp garlic powder
- 6 hamburger buns
- Coleslaw (optional)

Fun Facts

Pulled pork is a traditional Southern dish, often served at barbecues and gatherings.

Tender pulled pork smothered in smoky barbecue sauce, piled high on buns. Perfect for a summer cookout.

Directions

1. Place the pork roast in a slow cooker.
2. In a bowl, mix barbecue sauce, apple cider vinegar, brown sugar, smoked paprika, and garlic powder.
3. Pour the sauce over the pork.
4. Cook on low for 8 hours or until the pork is tender and easily shreds.
5. Shred the pork using two forks.
6. Serve on buns, topped with coleslaw if desired.
7. Enjoy!

4
servings

320

25 mins

Teriyaki Beef Stir-Fry

This teriyaki beef stir-fry is quick, easy, and bursting with sweet and savory flavors.

Ingredients:

- 1 lb flank steak (sliced thinly against the grain)
- 2 cups broccoli florets
- 1 red bell pepper (sliced)
- 1/2 cup teriyaki sauce
- 2 tbsp vegetable oil
- 2 cloves garlic (minced)
- 1 tsp ginger (minced)
- Cooked rice (for serving)

Directions

1. Heat vegetable oil in a large skillet or wok over high heat.
2. Add sliced beef and stir-fry for 2-3 mins until browned.
3. Add garlic and ginger, cook for another 30 seconds.
4. Add broccoli and red bell pepper, stir-fry for 2-3 mins until vegetables are tender-crisp.
5. Pour teriyaki sauce over the mixture.
6. Stir-fry for an additional 2 mins.
7. Serve over cooked rice.
8. Enjoy!

Fun Facts

Teriyaki sauce originated in Japan and is known for its sweet and salty flavor profile.

4
servings

280

20 mins

Honey Mustard Glazed Salmon

This salmon dish is a harmonious blend of sweet and tangy honey mustard glaze, perfectly complementing the rich salmon.

Ingredients:

- 4 salmon fillets
- 1/4 cup honey
- 2 tbsp Dijon mustard
- 1 tbsp whole grain mustard
- 1 tbsp olive oil
- 2 cloves garlic (minced)
- 1 tsp lemon juice
- Salt and pepper to taste

Directions

1. Preheat oven to 375°F (190°C).
2. In a bowl, whisk together honey, Dijon mustard, whole grain mustard, olive oil, garlic, lemon juice, salt, and pepper.
3. Place salmon fillets on a baking sheet lined with parchment paper.
4. Brush the glaze over the salmon.
5. Bake for 15-20 mins or until the salmon flakes easily with a fork.
6. Serve hot.
7. Drizzle with extra glaze if desired.
8. Enjoy!

Fun Facts

Salmon is a rich source of omega-3 fatty acids, which are beneficial for heart health.

4
servings

350

25 mins

Garlic Butter Shrimp Linguine

This pasta dish is a decadent delight with plump shrimp and linguine coated in a luscious garlic butter sauce.

Ingredients:

- 8 oz linguine pasta
- 1 lb large shrimp (peeled and deveined)
- 4 cloves garlic (minced)
- 1/4 cup unsalted butter
- 1/4 cup white wine (optional)
- 1/4 cup heavy cream
- 2 tbsp fresh parsley (chopped)
- Salt and pepper to taste

Directions

1. Cook linguine according to package instructions, then drain and set aside.
2. In a large skillet, melt butter over medium heat.
3. Add garlic and sauté for 1-2 mins until fragrant.
4. Add shrimp and cook until pink, about 2-3 mins per side.
5. Pour in white wine (if using) and simmer for 2 mins.
6. Stir in heavy cream, salt, and pepper.
7. Add cooked linguine and toss to coat.
8. Garnish with fresh parsley.
9. Serve hot.
10. Enjoy!

Fun Facts

Shrimp linguine is a classic Italian pasta dish that's known for its simple yet flavorful preparation.

4 servings

350

35 mins

Bacon-Wrapped Chicken Breast

Ingredients:

- 4 boneless, skinless chicken breasts
- 8 slices bacon
- 1/4 cup brown sugar
- 1 tsp paprika
- 1/2 tsp garlic powder
- 1/2 tsp onion powder
- Salt and pepper to taste

Indulge in this savory masterpiece of juicy chicken breasts wrapped in crispy bacon. A true crowd-pleaser.

Directions

1. Preheat oven to 375°F (190°C).
2. In a bowl, mix brown sugar, paprika, garlic powder, onion powder, salt, and pepper.
3. Wrap each chicken breast with 2 slices of bacon, securing with toothpicks.
4. Sprinkle the sugar-spice mixture over the chicken.
5. Place chicken on a baking sheet.
6. Bake for 30-35 mins or until chicken is cooked through.
7. Remove toothpicks before serving.
8. Enjoy!

Fun Facts

Bacon-wrapped dishes are a popular party favorite, loved for their combination of savory and salty flavors.

4
servings

280

30 mins

Balsamic Glazed Pork Chops

Ingredients:

- 4 bone-in pork chops
- 1/4 cup balsamic vinegar
- 1/4 cup honey
- 2 cloves garlic (minced)
- 1/2 tsp dried thyme
- Salt and pepper to taste

These pork chops are seared to perfection and glazed with a balsamic reduction, creating a sweet and tangy masterpiece.

Directions

1. Season pork chops with salt and pepper.
2. In a skillet, heat olive oil over medium-high heat.
3. Sear pork chops for 4-5 mins per side or until browned and cooked through.
4. Remove pork chops and set aside.
5. In the same skillet, add minced garlic and sauté for 1 min.
6. Stir in balsamic vinegar, honey, and dried thyme.
7. Simmer until the glaze thickens, about 3-4 mins.
8. Return pork chops to the skillet and coat with the glaze.
9. Serve hot.
10. Enjoy!

Fun Facts

Balsamic vinegar is aged in wooden barrels, and the older it is, the thicker and sweeter it becomes.

4
servings

350

25 mins

Beef and Broccoli Stir-Fry

Ingredients:

- 1 lb flank steak (sliced thinly against the grain)
- 4 cups broccoli florets
- 1/2 cup beef broth
- 1/4 cup soy sauce
- 2 tbsp brown sugar
- 1 tbsp cornstarch
- 2 cloves garlic (minced)
- 1 tsp ginger (minced)
- 2 tbsp vegetable oil
- Cooked rice (for serving)

Fun Facts

Beef and broccoli stir-fry is a classic Chinese-American dish that's popular for its savory flavors and quick preparation.

This stir-fry is a quick and nutritious dish featuring tender beef and vibrant broccoli in a savory sauce.

Directions

1. In a bowl, whisk together beef broth, soy sauce, brown sugar, and cornstarch.
2. Heat vegetable oil in a large skillet or wok over high heat.
3. Add sliced beef and stir-fry for 2-3 mins until browned.
4. Add garlic and ginger, cook for another 30 seconds.
5. Add broccoli and stir-fry for 2-3 mins until vegetables are tender-crisp.
6. Pour the sauce over the mixture and stir until thickened.
7. Serve over cooked rice.
8. Enjoy!

6
servings

300

2 hours

Maple Dijon Glazed Ham

Ingredients:

- 4-6 lb bone-in ham
- 1/2 cup maple syrup
- 1/4 cup Dijon mustard
- 1/4 cup brown sugar
- 2 cloves garlic (minced)
- 1 tsp ground cloves
- Salt and pepper to taste

Fun Facts

Glazed ham is a popular dish for holiday feasts, particularly Easter and Christmas.

A succulent ham glazed with a sweet and tangy mixture of maple syrup and Dijon mustard. Perfect for festive occasions.

Directions

1. Preheat oven to 325°F (163°C).
2. Score the surface of the ham in a diamond pattern.
3. In a bowl, whisk together maple syrup, Dijon mustard, brown sugar, minced garlic, ground cloves, salt, and pepper.
4. Brush the glaze over the ham.
5. Place ham in a roasting pan and cover with foil.
6. Bake for 1 hour and 30 mins, basting with glaze every 30 mins.
7. Remove foil for the last 30 mins to allow the ham to brown.
8. Let it rest for 10 mins before slicing.
9. Enjoy!

4
servings

250

30 mins

Herbed Grilled Pork Tenderloin

A tender and flavorful pork tenderloin marinated with a blend of herbs and grilled to perfection. A true summer delight.

Ingredients:

- 1 lb pork tenderloin
- 2 cloves garlic (minced)
- 2 tbsp fresh rosemary (chopped)
- 2 tbsp fresh thyme (chopped)
- 2 tbsp olive oil
- 1 tbsp Dijon mustard
- 1 tbsp lemon juice
- Salt and pepper to taste

Directions

1. In a bowl, mix garlic, rosemary, thyme, olive oil, Dijon mustard, lemon juice, salt, and pepper.
2. Rub the mixture over the pork tenderloin.
3. Let it marinate for at least 15 mins, or refrigerate for a few hours for more flavor.
4. Preheat the grill to medium-high heat.
5. Grill the pork for 20-25 mins, turning occasionally, until the internal temperature reaches 145°F (63°C).
6. Let it rest for 5 mins before slicing.
7. Serve hot.
8. Enjoy!

Fun Facts

Pork tenderloin is one of the leanest cuts of pork and is known for its tenderness and mild flavor.

Chapter 4:
Poultry Perfection

4
servings

450

30 mins

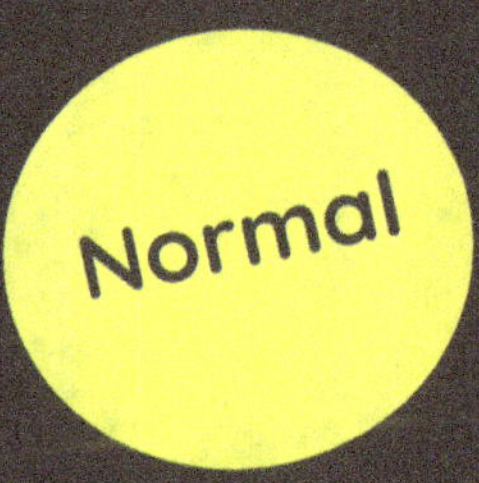

Creamy Chicken Alfredo

Indulge in the luxurious flavors of this creamy chicken Alfredo pasta, a classic Italian dish with tender chicken and a rich sauce.

Ingredients:

- 8 oz fettuccine pasta
- 2 boneless, skinless chicken breasts (sliced)
- 2 cloves garlic (minced)
- 1/4 cup unsalted butter
- 1 cup heavy cream
- 1 cup grated Parmesan cheese
- 1/4 cup fresh parsley (chopped)
- Salt and pepper to taste

Directions

1. Cook fettuccine pasta according to package instructions, then drain and set aside.
2. Season chicken slices with salt and pepper.
3. In a large skillet, melt butter over medium-high heat.
4. Add chicken and cook until no longer pink, about 5 mins per side.
5. Remove chicken from the skillet.
6. In the same skillet, add minced garlic and sauté for 1 min.
7. Pour in heavy cream, Parmesan cheese, salt, and pepper.
8. Simmer for 5 mins until the sauce thickens.
9. Return cooked chicken to the skillet.
10. Add cooked pasta and toss to coat.
11. Garnish with fresh parsley.
12. Serve hot.
13. Enjoy!

Fun Facts

Alfredo sauce is named after Alfredo di Lelio, an Italian restaurateur who created the dish to please his pregnant wife.

4 servings

280

2 hours

Lemon Herb Roasted Turkey Breast

Ingredients:

- 2.5 lbs boneless turkey breast
- Zest and juice of 1 lemon
- 2 cloves garlic (minced)
- 2 tbsp fresh rosemary (chopped)
- 2 tbsp fresh thyme (chopped)
- 2 tbsp olive oil
- Salt and pepper to taste

Fun Facts

Roasting turkey breast is a great option for smaller gatherings or when you want a quicker turkey dish.

This roasted turkey breast is a flavorful and succulent centerpiece for your holiday table, infused with zesty lemon and aromatic herbs.

Directions

1. Preheat oven to 325°F (163°C).
2. In a bowl, mix lemon zest, lemon juice, garlic, rosemary, thyme, olive oil, salt, and pepper.
3. Place turkey breast in a roasting pan.
4. Brush the herb and lemon mixture over the turkey.
5. Roast in the oven for 1 hour and 45 mins or until the internal temperature reaches 165°F (74°C).
6. Let it rest for 10 mins before slicing.
7. Serve hot.
8. Enjoy!

4
servings

350

35 mins

Honey Garlic Chicken Thighs

These honey garlic chicken thighs are sticky, sweet, and savory. A finger-licking good dish that's simple to make.

Ingredients:

- 8 bone-in, skin-on chicken thighs
- 1/4 cup honey
- 1/4 cup soy sauce
- 3 cloves garlic (minced)
- 1 tsp grated ginger
- 1 tsp sesame oil
- Salt and pepper to taste

Directions

1. Preheat oven to 375°F (190°C).
2. Season chicken thighs with salt and pepper.
3. In a bowl, mix honey, soy sauce, minced garlic, grated ginger, and sesame oil.
4. Place chicken thighs in a baking dish.
5. Pour the honey garlic sauce over the chicken.
6. Bake for 30-35 mins, basting with the sauce every 10 mins, until chicken is cooked through and skin is crispy.
7. Serve hot.
8. Enjoy!

Fun Facts

Honey garlic chicken is a popular dish in Chinese cuisine and is known for its sweet and savory flavors.

4
servings

320

30 mins

Chicken Fajita Wraps

Ingredients:

- 2 boneless, skinless chicken breasts (sliced)
- 1 red bell pepper (sliced)
- 1 green bell pepper (sliced)
- 1 onion (sliced)
- 2 cloves garlic (minced)
- 2 tbsp olive oil
- 2 tsp chili powder
- 1 tsp cumin
- Salt and pepper to taste
- 4 large flour tortillas

Fun Facts

Fajitas are a Tex-Mex dish that originated in the ranchlands of West Texas, made with sizzling grilled meat and veggies.

These chicken fajita wraps are bursting with Mexican flavors. Tender chicken, colorful bell peppers, and onions make for a delicious meal.

Directions

1. In a bowl, mix sliced chicken, minced garlic, chili powder, cumin, salt, and pepper.
2. In a large skillet, heat olive oil over medium-high heat.
3. Add chicken and cook until no longer pink, about 5 mins per side.
4. Remove chicken from the skillet.
5. In the same skillet, add sliced bell peppers and onions.
6. Sauté until vegetables are tender-crisp, about 5 mins.
7. Return cooked chicken to the skillet and toss with the vegetables.
8. Warm tortillas in the oven or on a griddle.
9. Serve chicken and vegetable mixture on tortillas.
10. Roll up and enjoy!

4
servings

280

45 mins

Teriyaki Chicken Drumsticks

Ingredients:

- 12 chicken drumsticks
- 1/2 cup soy sauce
- 1/4 cup mirin (Japanese sweet rice wine)
- 1/4 cup sake (Japanese rice wine, or white wine)
- 1/4 cup brown sugar
- 2 cloves garlic (minced)
- 1 tsp grated ginger
- Sesame seeds and chopped green onions (for garnish)

Fun Facts

Teriyaki sauce is a Japanese cooking technique that involves grilling or broiling food with a glaze made from soy sauce, mirin, and sugar.

These teriyaki chicken drumsticks are sticky, sweet, and savory. A crowd-pleaser that's perfect for a family dinner or party.

Directions

1. In a bowl, mix soy sauce, mirin, sake, brown sugar, minced garlic, and grated ginger to make the teriyaki sauce.
2. Place chicken drumsticks in a large resealable bag.
3. Pour half of the teriyaki sauce into the bag with the chicken.
4. Seal the bag and marinate in the refrigerator for at least 30 mins, or up to 4 hours.
5. Preheat oven to 375°F (190°C).
6. Place marinated chicken drumsticks on a baking sheet lined with foil.
7. Bake for 30-35 mins, turning and basting with the remaining teriyaki sauce every 10 mins, until chicken is cooked through and glazed.
8. Garnish with sesame seeds and chopped green onions.
9. Serve hot.
10. Enjoy!

4
servings

350

40 mins

Pesto Stuffed Chicken Breast

Ingredients:

- 4 boneless, skinless chicken breasts
- 1/2 cup pesto sauce
- 1 cup shredded mozzarella cheese
- 1 tbsp olive oil
- Salt and pepper to taste

Fun Facts

Pesto, originally from Italy, is a versatile sauce made from fresh basil, pine nuts, garlic, Parmesan cheese, and olive oil.

These chicken breasts are stuffed with aromatic pesto and creamy mozzarella cheese, creating a delightful and flavorful dish.

Directions

1. Preheat oven to 375°F (190°C).
2. Cut a slit in each chicken breast to create a pocket for stuffing.
3. Season chicken breasts with salt and pepper.
4. Stuff each chicken breast with 2 tbsp of pesto sauce and 1/4 cup of shredded mozzarella cheese.
5. Heat olive oil in an ovenproof skillet over medium-high heat.
6. Sear chicken breasts for 2-3 mins per side until browned.
7. Transfer skillet to the preheated oven and bake for 20-25 mins or until chicken is cooked through and cheese is melted and bubbly.
8. Serve hot.
9. Enjoy!

4
servings

320

40 mins

Maple Glazed Chicken Wings

Ingredients:

- 2 lbs chicken wings
- 1/4 cup maple syrup
- 2 tbsp soy sauce
- 2 cloves garlic (minced)
- 1 tsp Dijon mustard
- Salt and pepper to taste

Fun Facts

Chicken wings are a popular snack and appetizer, often enjoyed at parties and sports events.

These maple glazed chicken wings are sweet, sticky, and finger-licking good. Perfect for game day or as a tasty appetizer.

Directions

1. Preheat oven to 425°F (218°C).
2. Season chicken wings with salt and pepper.
3. In a bowl, mix maple syrup, soy sauce, minced garlic, and Dijon mustard to make the glaze.
4. Place chicken wings on a baking sheet lined with foil.
5. Brush the glaze over the chicken wings.
6. Bake for 35-40 mins, turning and basting with the glaze every 15 mins, until wings are cooked through and glazed.
7. Serve hot.
8. Enjoy!

4
servings

380

30 mins

BBQ Chicken Pizza

This BBQ chicken pizza is a mouthwatering combination of smoky barbecue sauce, tender chicken, and melted cheese on a crispy crust.

Ingredients:

- 1 (12-inch) pizza crust (store-bought or homemade)
- 1/2 cup barbecue sauce
- 1.5 cups cooked chicken (shredded)
- 1 cup shredded mozzarella cheese
- 1/2 red onion (thinly sliced)
- 1/4 cup fresh cilantro (chopped)
- Olive oil (for drizzling)
- Salt and pepper to taste

Directions

1. Preheat oven to the temperature specified for your pizza crust (usually around 425°F or 220°C).
2. Roll out the pizza dough on a baking sheet or pizza stone.
3. Spread barbecue sauce evenly over the pizza dough.
4. Sprinkle shredded chicken over the sauce.
5. Top with shredded mozzarella cheese and thinly sliced red onion.
6. Drizzle olive oil over the pizza and season with salt and pepper.
7. Bake according to your pizza crust instructions until the crust is golden and the cheese is bubbly and browned, usually 15-20 mins.
8. Remove from the oven and sprinkle with fresh cilantro.
9. Slice and serve hot.
10. Enjoy!

Fun Facts

BBQ chicken pizza is a popular variation of pizza that incorporates the flavors of barbecue sauce and grilled chicken.

4 servings

320 kcal

30 mins

Garlic Butter Chicken Skillet

Ingredients:

- 4 boneless, skinless chicken breasts
- 4 cloves garlic (minced)
- 1/4 cup unsalted butter
- 1/2 cup chicken broth
- 1/2 cup heavy cream
- 1/4 cup grated Parmesan cheese
- 2 tbsp fresh parsley (chopped)
- Salt and pepper to taste

Fun Facts

Garlic butter sauce is a versatile and beloved condiment used in many savory dishes, such as pasta and seafood.

This garlic butter chicken skillet is a one-pan wonder, with tender chicken in a luscious garlic butter sauce. A comforting and satisfying meal.

Directions

1. Season chicken breasts with salt and pepper.
2. In a large skillet, melt butter over medium-high heat.
3. Add chicken and cook until golden brown and no longer pink in the center, about 6-7 mins per side.
4. Remove chicken from the skillet and set aside.
5. In the same skillet, add minced garlic and sauté for 1 min until fragrant.
6. Pour in chicken broth, heavy cream, and grated Parmesan cheese.
7. Simmer for 5 mins until the sauce thickens.
8. Return cooked chicken to the skillet and coat with the garlic butter sauce.
9. Garnish with fresh parsley.
10. Serve hot.
11. Enjoy!

4
servings

380

30 mins

Orange Ginger Duck Breast

Ingredients:

- 4 duck breast halves
- Zest and juice of 2 oranges
- 2 tbsp soy sauce
- 1 tbsp honey
- 1 tsp grated ginger
- 2 cloves garlic (minced)
- Salt and pepper to taste

Fun Facts

Duck breast is known for its rich, flavorful meat, and it pairs beautifully with citrusy and savory glazes.

This duck breast is a symphony of flavors, with a zesty orange and ginger glaze that perfectly complements the rich, tender meat.

Directions

1. Season duck breast halves with salt and pepper.
2. In a bowl, mix orange zest, orange juice, soy sauce, honey, grated ginger, and minced garlic to make the glaze.
3. Preheat a skillet over medium-high heat.
4. Place duck breasts in the skillet, skin side down, and sear for 4-5 mins until skin is crispy and browned.
5. Flip the duck breasts and cook for an additional 3-4 mins, or until desired doneness.
6. Remove duck from the skillet and let it rest for 5 mins.
7. Slice the duck.
8. Drizzle with the orange ginger glaze.
9. Serve hot.
10. Enjoy!

We have a small favor to ask

Midway through your culinary exploration of "Weeknight Wonders: A 5-Ingredient Cookbook," we hope you've already savored some mouthwatering dishes and found the ease and simplicity of our recipes a delightful revelation.

As you immerse yourself in the world of quick dinner ideas and easy weeknight meals, we'd like to take a moment to talk about something essential to the life of a cookbook: reviews. Yes, those little stars and thoughtful comments you see on your favorite culinary guides. They're more than just words; they are the lifeblood of authors and small, passionate publishers like us.

You see, reviews are as hard to come by as a perfectly cooked soufflé. They're the seasoning that adds flavor to the wonderful dish that is this cookbook. Your reviews serve as signposts to fellow culinary explorers, helping them find the recipes that will delight their taste buds and simplify their lives. A review from you is like a secret ingredient, a hidden gem that can make this cookbook shine even brighter.

So, if you're enjoying the recipes, finding them as practical and scrumptious as we intended, and you think, "I'd like to tell others about this," please consider going back to the platform where you obtained this cookbook. Click on the review button and share your honest thoughts. A simple star rating and a short sentence or two about your experience can make all the difference in helping this cookbook find its way into the kitchens of those seeking a solution to weeknight meal dilemmas.

We read each review with genuine appreciation and keen interest. Your feedback helps us shape the direction of our culinary journey and guides us in our mission to make home cooking a delightful and accessible experience for everyone.

In a cookbook, just as in life, there might be a few imperfections and hiccups along the way. We strive for perfection in every recipe, but the occasional misstep is a part of our journey. Your constructive feedback is the compass that keeps us on course and enables us to continually improve our recipes.

As you return to your culinary adventure, we invite you to remember the power of your voice in this vast world of flavors. Your words matter, and they can inspire others to embark on their own culinary journey, even on the busiest of weeknights.

Thank you for choosing "Weeknight Wonders: A 5-Ingredient Cookbook" as your culinary companion. Your trust in our recipes and your engagement in this gastronomic adventure inspire us to continue sharing the joy of cooking with you.

Now, let's get back to the heart of this book – the recipes that make weeknight cooking a true wonder. Enjoy, savor, and experiment with the delightful simplicity of these dishes. There's more culinary magic to uncover, and we're thrilled to have you with us.

Chapter 5:
Seafood Sensations

4
servings

320

25 mins

Garlic Butter
Shrimp Scampi

Ingredients:

- 1 lb large shrimp (peeled and deveined)
- 8 oz linguine pasta
- 4 cloves garlic (minced)
- 1/4 cup unsalted butter
- 1/4 cup white wine (optional)
- Juice of 1 lemon
- Zest of 1 lemon
- 2 tbsp fresh parsley (chopped)
- Red pepper flakes (optional, for heat)
- Salt and pepper to taste

Fun Facts

Shrimp scampi is a classic Italian-American dish known for its bold garlic and buttery flavors.

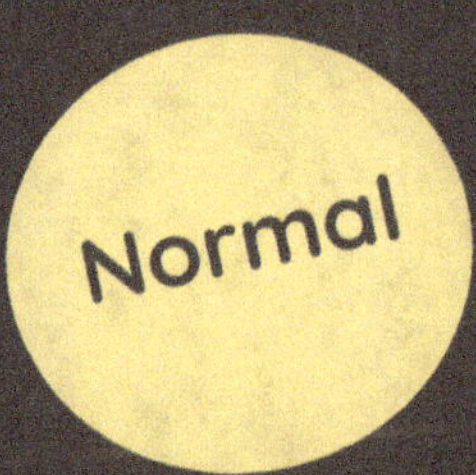

Dive into the flavors of this garlic butter shrimp scampi. Plump shrimp are cooked in a luscious garlic butter sauce, making it a quick and elegant dish.

Directions

1. Cook linguine pasta according to package instructions, then drain and set aside.
2. Season shrimp with salt and pepper.
3. In a large skillet, melt butter over medium-high heat.
4. Add minced garlic and cook for 1 min until fragrant.
5. Add shrimp and cook for 2-3 mins until pink, turning once.
6. If using, pour in white wine and simmer for 2 mins.
7. Stir in lemon juice, lemon zest, and red pepper flakes (if using).
8. Add cooked linguine to the skillet and toss to coat in the garlic butter sauce.
9. Garnish with fresh parsley.
10. Serve hot.
11. Enjoy!

4
servings

300

30 mins

Baked Lemon Dill Salmon

Ingredients:

- 4 salmon fillets
- Zest and juice of 1 lemon
- 2 cloves garlic (minced)
- 2 tbsp fresh dill (chopped)
- 2 tbsp olive oil
- Salt and pepper to taste

This baked salmon is a light and flavorful dish, featuring tender salmon fillets infused with the brightness of lemon and the freshness of dill.

Directions

1. Preheat oven to 375°F (190°C).
2. Season salmon fillets with salt and pepper.
3. In a bowl, mix lemon zest, lemon juice, minced garlic, fresh dill, and olive oil.
4. Place salmon fillets on a baking sheet lined with parchment paper.
5. Brush the lemon dill mixture over the salmon.
6. Bake for 15-20 mins or until the salmon flakes easily with a fork.
7. Serve hot.
8. Enjoy!

Fun Facts

Salmon is a rich source of omega-3 fatty acids, which are beneficial for heart health.

**4
servings**

280

20 mins

Cajun Grilled Tilapia

Ingredients:

- 4 tilapia fillets
- 2 tbsp Cajun seasoning
- 2 tbsp olive oil
- 1 lemon (cut into wedges)
- Salt and pepper to taste

Spice up your dinner with Cajun grilled tilapia. The smoky and spicy flavors of Cajun seasoning make this dish a delightful treat.

Directions

1. Preheat grill to medium-high heat.
2. Season tilapia fillets with salt, pepper, and Cajun seasoning.
3. Drizzle olive oil over the fillets.
4. Place tilapia on the grill and cook for 4-5 mins per side or until fish flakes easily with a fork.
5. Serve hot with lemon wedges.
6. Enjoy!

Fun Facts

Cajun cuisine originated in Louisiana and is known for its bold and spicy flavors.

4
servings

350

35 mins

Coconut Curry Shrimp

Enjoy the exotic flavors of coconut curry shrimp. Succulent shrimp are simmered in a creamy coconut sauce with aromatic spices for a delightful twist.

Ingredients:

- 1 lb large shrimp (peeled and deveined)
- 1 can (13.5 oz) coconut milk
- 2 tbsp red curry paste
- 1 red bell pepper (sliced)
- 1 onion (sliced)
- 2 cloves garlic (minced)
- 1 tsp grated ginger
- 2 tbsp vegetable oil
- 2 tbsp fresh cilantro (chopped)
- Salt and pepper to taste

Directions

1. Heat vegetable oil in a large skillet over medium-high heat.
2. Add sliced onion and red bell pepper, and sauté for 2-3 mins until softened.
3. Add minced garlic and grated ginger, and cook for 1 min until fragrant.
4. Stir in red curry paste and cook for 1 min.
5. Pour in coconut milk and bring to a simmer.
6. Add shrimp and simmer for 4-5 mins until shrimp are pink and cooked through.
7. Season with salt and pepper.
8. Garnish with fresh cilantro.
9. Serve hot.
10. Enjoy!

Fun Facts

Coconut curry is a popular dish in many Southeast Asian cuisines, known for its rich and fragrant flavors.

4
servings

290

25 mins

Blackened Catfish Fillets

These blackened catfish fillets are a spicy Southern delight. A bold seasoning blend creates a flavorful crust on tender catfish.

Ingredients:

- 4 catfish fillets
- 2 tbsp paprika
- 1 tsp dried thyme
- 1 tsp dried oregano
- 1 tsp garlic powder
- 1 tsp onion powder
- 1/2 tsp cayenne pepper
- 1/2 tsp salt
- 1/4 tsp black pepper
- 2 tbsp butter
- Lemon wedges (for serving)

Directions

1. In a bowl, mix paprika, dried thyme, dried oregano, garlic powder, onion powder, cayenne pepper, salt, and black pepper to create the blackening seasoning.
2. Pat catfish fillets dry with paper towels.
3. Coat each fillet generously with the blackening seasoning mixture.
4. In a large skillet, heat butter over medium-high heat.
5. Add catfish fillets and cook for 3-4 mins per side until fish flakes easily with a fork and the crust is blackened and crispy.
6. Serve hot with lemon wedges.
7. Enjoy!

Fun Facts

Blackened catfish is a classic dish from Louisiana, known for its spicy and smoky flavors.

4 servings

320

15 mins

Lemon Butter Scallops

Ingredients:

- 1 lb sea scallops
- 2 cloves garlic (minced)
- Zest and juice of 1 lemon
- 2 tbsp unsalted butter
- 2 tbsp fresh parsley (chopped)
- Salt and pepper to taste

Fun Facts

Scallops are often considered a delicacy and are known for their tender and sweet meat.

These lemon butter scallops are a quick and elegant seafood dish. Tender scallops are seared to perfection in a zesty lemon butter sauce.

Directions

1. Pat scallops dry with paper towels and season with salt and pepper.
2. Heat a skillet over medium-high heat.
3. Add scallops and sear for 2-3 mins per side until golden brown and opaque in the center.
4. Remove scallops from the skillet and set aside.
5. In the same skillet, add minced garlic and cook for 1 min until fragrant.
6. Stir in lemon zest, lemon juice, and unsalted butter.
7. Simmer for 2-3 mins until the sauce thickens.
8. Return scallops to the skillet and coat with the lemon butter sauce.
9. Garnish with fresh parsley.
10. Serve hot.
11. Enjoy!

4 servings **340** **35 mins**

Teriyaki Glazed Tuna Steaks

Ingredients:

- 4 tuna steaks
- 1/2 cup soy sauce
- 1/4 cup mirin (Japanese sweet rice wine)
- 1/4 cup sake (Japanese rice wine, or white wine)
- 1/4 cup brown sugar
- 2 cloves garlic (minced)
- 1 tsp grated ginger
- 1 tsp sesame oil
- Sesame seeds (for garnish)
- Green onions (for garnish)
- Salt and pepper to taste

Fun Facts

Tuna steaks are a popular choice for grilling and searing, known for their meaty texture and rich flavor.

These teriyaki glazed tuna steaks are a culinary masterpiece. Succulent tuna is marinated in a sweet and savory teriyaki sauce, then seared to perfection.

Directions

1. In a bowl, mix soy sauce, mirin, sake, brown sugar, minced garlic, grated ginger, and sesame oil to make the teriyaki sauce.
2. Season tuna steaks with salt and pepper.
3. Place tuna steaks in a resealable bag and pour half of the teriyaki sauce over them.
4. Seal the bag and marinate in the refrigerator for at least 30 mins, or up to 4 hours.
5. Preheat a skillet or grill pan over high heat.
6. Remove tuna steaks from the marinade and discard the marinade.
7. Sear tuna steaks for 1-2 mins per side for rare, or longer for desired doneness.
8. Garnish with sesame seeds and chopped green onions.
9. Serve hot.
10. Enjoy!

4
servings

280

25 mins

Garlic Herb Baked Cod

This garlic herb baked cod is a simple and flavorful seafood dish. Cod fillets are baked with a fragrant garlic herb butter sauce for a delightful meal.

Ingredients:

- 4 cod fillets
- 2 cloves garlic (minced)
- 2 tbsp unsalted butter
- 2 tbsp fresh parsley (chopped)
- 1 tbsp fresh dill (chopped)
- 1 lemon (cut into wedges)
- Salt and pepper to taste

Directions

1. Preheat oven to 400°F (200°C).
2. Season cod fillets with salt and pepper.
3. In a small saucepan, melt unsalted butter over low heat.
4. Add minced garlic and sauté for 1 min until fragrant.
5. Stir in fresh parsley and fresh dill.
6. Place cod fillets on a baking sheet lined with parchment paper.
7. Brush the garlic herb butter sauce over the cod fillets.
8. Bake for 12-15 mins or until the cod flakes easily with a fork.
9. Serve hot with lemon wedges.
10. Enjoy!

Fun Facts

Cod is a mild and flaky white fish that is often used in baked and grilled dishes.

4
servings

250

30 mins

Spicy Sriracha Tofu

Ingredients:

- 1 lb extra-firm tofu (cubed)
- 2 tbsp Sriracha sauce (adjust to taste)
- 2 tbsp soy sauce
- 1 tbsp honey
- 1 tbsp vegetable oil
- 1 tsp sesame seeds (for garnish)
- Green onions (for garnish)
- Salt and pepper to taste

Fun Facts

Sriracha sauce is a popular Thai hot sauce known for its spicy and tangy flavor.

Spice up your meal with this spicy Sriracha tofu. Crispy tofu cubes are coated in a fiery Sriracha sauce for a bold and flavorful dish.

Directions

1. Preheat oven to 400°F (200°C).
2. Season tofu cubes with salt and pepper.
3. Place tofu on a baking sheet lined with parchment paper.
4. Bake for 25-30 mins, turning halfway through, until tofu is crispy and golden brown.
5. In a bowl, mix Sriracha sauce, soy sauce, honey, and vegetable oil to make the spicy sauce.
6. Toss baked tofu cubes in the spicy Sriracha sauce.
7. Garnish with sesame seeds and chopped green onions.
8. Serve hot.
9. Enjoy!

4
servings

380

35 mins

Creamy Garlic Butter Lobster Tails

Ingredients:

- 4 lobster tails
- 4 cloves garlic (minced)
- 1/2 cup unsalted butter
- 1/4 cup heavy cream
- 1/4 cup grated Parmesan cheese
- 2 tbsp fresh parsley (chopped)
- Salt and pepper to taste

Fun Facts

Lobster tails are a luxurious seafood delicacy, often enjoyed on special occasions.

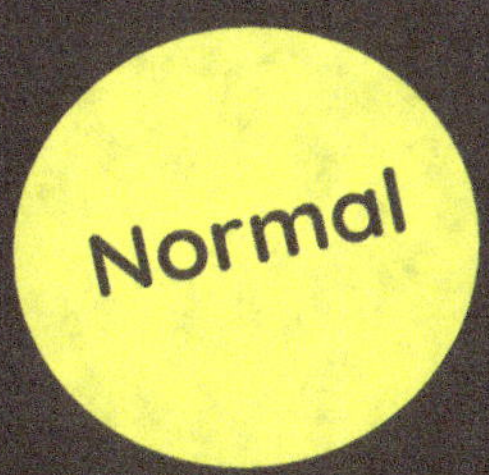

Indulge in the decadence of creamy garlic butter lobster tails. Lobster tails are bathed in a rich and velvety garlic butter sauce for an exquisite dining experience.

Directions

1. Preheat oven to 425°F (218°C).
2. Use kitchen shears to cut the top of each lobster tail lengthwise and lift the meat slightly.
3. Season lobster tails with salt and pepper.
4. In a saucepan, melt unsalted butter over low heat.
5. Add minced garlic and sauté for 1 min until fragrant.
6. Stir in heavy cream and grated Parmesan cheese.
7. Simmer for 2-3 mins until the sauce thickens.
8. Place lobster tails on a baking sheet.
9. Spoon the garlic butter sauce over the lobster tails.
10. Bake for 10-12 mins until lobster meat is opaque and cooked through.
11. Garnish with fresh parsley.
12. Serve hot.
13. Enjoy!

Chapter 6:
Veggie Delights

4
servings

350

40 mins

Creamy Mushroom Risotto

Ingredients:

- 1.5 cups Arborio rice
- 8 oz mushrooms (sliced)
- 4 cups vegetable broth
- 1 cup dry white wine (optional)
- 1 onion (finely chopped)
- 2 cloves garlic (minced)
- 2 tbsp olive oil
- 1/2 cup grated Parmesan cheese
- 2 tbsp fresh parsley (chopped)
- Salt and pepper to taste

Fun Facts

Risotto is an Italian rice dish known for its creamy texture achieved through gradual addition of broth.

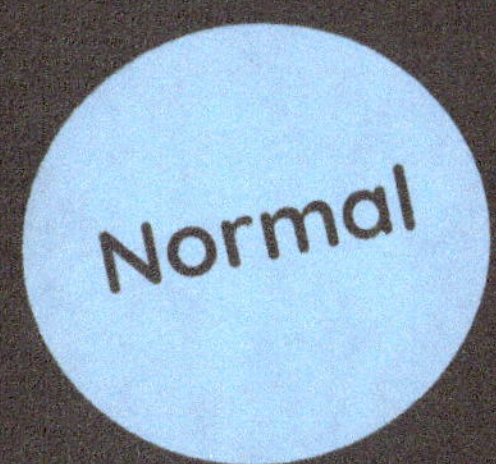

Savor the indulgence of creamy mushroom risotto. Arborio rice is cooked to perfection in a rich and velvety mushroom broth, creating a comforting and elegant dish.

Directions

1. In a saucepan, heat vegetable broth and keep it warm over low heat.
2. In a large skillet, heat olive oil over medium-high heat.
3. Add chopped onion and sauté for 2-3 mins until translucent.
4. Stir in minced garlic and cook for 1 min until fragrant.
5. Add Arborio rice and cook for 2 mins, stirring frequently until rice is translucent at the edges.
6. If using, pour in white wine and simmer until it's mostly absorbed by the rice.
7. Add sliced mushrooms and cook for 3-4 mins until they release their moisture and become tender.
8. Begin adding the warm vegetable broth, one ladle at a time, stirring constantly and allowing the liquid to be absorbed before adding more.
9. Continue this process for about 20-25 mins or until the rice is creamy and tender with a slight bite.
10. Stir in grated Parmesan cheese.
11. Season with salt and pepper to taste.
12. Garnish with fresh parsley.
13. Serve hot.
14. Enjoy!

4 servings

150 kcal

20 mins

Roasted Asparagus with Parmesan

Ingredients:

- 1 lb fresh asparagus spears
- 2 tbsp olive oil
- 1/4 cup grated Parmesan cheese
- 2 cloves garlic (minced)
- Salt and pepper to taste

Fun Facts

Asparagus is a low-calorie vegetable packed with vitamins and minerals, making it a healthy choice.

Elevate your meal with roasted asparagus with Parmesan. Fresh asparagus spears are roasted to perfection, then topped with savory Parmesan cheese for a delightful side dish.

Directions

1. Preheat oven to 425°F (218°C).
2. Trim the tough ends of the asparagus spears.
3. Place asparagus on a baking sheet lined with parchment paper.
4. Drizzle olive oil over the asparagus and toss to coat.
5. Sprinkle minced garlic, grated Parmesan cheese, salt, and pepper over the asparagus.
6. Roast in the preheated oven for 12-15 mins, or until asparagus is tender and slightly crispy at the tips.
7. Serve hot.
8. Enjoy!

4
servings

280

45 mins

Spinach and Ricotta Stuffed Bell Peppers

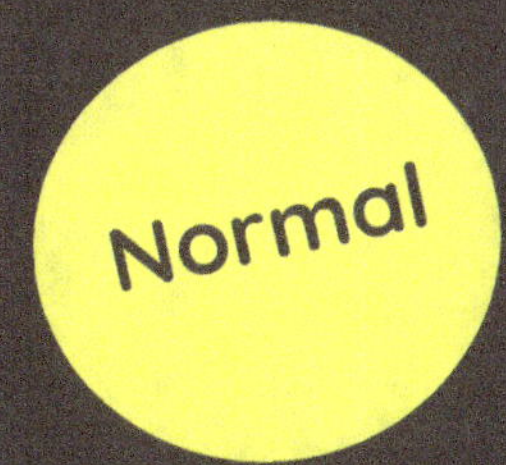

Ingredients:

- 4 bell peppers (any color)
- 2 cups fresh spinach (chopped)
- 1 cup ricotta cheese
- 1/2 cup grated Parmesan cheese
- 1/4 cup fresh basil (chopped)
- 2 cloves garlic (minced)
- 1/4 cup pine nuts (toasted)
- 2 tbsp olive oil
- Salt and pepper to taste

Enjoy the wholesome goodness of spinach and ricotta stuffed bell peppers. Bell peppers are filled with a flavorful mixture of spinach, ricotta cheese, and herbs, then baked to perfection.

Directions

1. Preheat oven to 375°F (190°C).
2. Cut the tops off the bell peppers and remove the seeds and membranes.
3. In a skillet, heat olive oil over medium-high heat.
4. Add minced garlic and cook for 1 min until fragrant.
5. Stir in chopped spinach and cook for 2-3 mins until wilted.
6. Remove from heat and let it cool slightly.
7. In a bowl, combine cooked spinach, ricotta cheese, grated Parmesan cheese, chopped fresh basil, and toasted pine nuts.
8. Season with salt and pepper to taste.
9. Stuff each bell pepper with the spinach and ricotta mixture.
10. Place stuffed bell peppers in a baking dish.
11. Cover with foil and bake for 25-30 mins, or until the peppers are tender.
12. Remove the foil and bake for an additional 5 mins until the tops are slightly browned.
13. Serve hot.
14. Enjoy!

Fun Facts

Stuffed bell peppers are a versatile dish that can be filled with a variety of ingredients and flavors.

4
servings

180

15 mins

Garlic Butter Green Beans

Ingredients:

- 1 lb fresh green beans (trimmed)
- 2 cloves garlic (minced)
- 2 tbsp unsalted butter
- 2 tbsp olive oil
- 1 tbsp fresh lemon juice
- Salt and pepper to taste

Elevate your green beans with garlic butter. Tender green beans are sautéed in a flavorful garlic butter sauce for a simple yet delicious side dish.

Directions

1. In a large skillet, heat olive oil and unsalted butter over medium-high heat.
2. Add minced garlic and sauté for 1 min until fragrant.
3. Add trimmed green beans to the skillet.
4. Sauté green beans for 5-7 mins, tossing frequently, until they are tender and slightly crispy.
5. Drizzle fresh lemon juice over the green beans.
6. Season with salt and pepper to taste.
7. Serve hot.
8. Enjoy!

Fun Facts

Green beans are a nutritious vegetable and a great source of vitamins and fiber.

4
servings

320

30 mins

Sweet Potato and Black Bean Tacos

Ingredients:

- 2 large sweet potatoes (peeled and diced)
- 1 can (15 oz) black beans (drained and rinsed)
- 2 tbsp olive oil
- 1 tsp chili powder
- 1 tsp ground cumin
- 1/2 tsp paprika
- 1/4 tsp cayenne pepper (optional, for heat)
- 8 small flour tortillas
- Toppings of your choice (salsa, avocado, sour cream, etc.)
- Salt and pepper to taste

Fun Facts

Sweet potatoes are a nutritious and flavorful addition to tacos, providing a natural sweetness.

Dive into the flavors of sweet potato and black bean tacos. Roasted sweet potatoes and seasoned black beans are tucked into warm tortillas and topped with your favorite taco fixings for a satisfying meal.

Directions

1. Preheat oven to 425°F (218°C).
2. In a bowl, toss diced sweet potatoes with olive oil, chili powder, ground cumin, paprika, and cayenne pepper (if using).
3. Spread sweet potatoes in a single layer on a baking sheet lined with parchment paper.
4. Roast for 20-25 mins, or until sweet potatoes are tender and slightly caramelized.
5. While the sweet potatoes are roasting, heat the drained and rinsed black beans in a saucepan over medium heat. Season with salt and pepper to taste.
6. Warm the flour tortillas according to package instructions.
7. Assemble tacos by placing a scoop of roasted sweet potatoes and a spoonful of black beans on each tortilla.
8. Top with your favorite taco toppings.
9. Serve hot.
10. Enjoy!

4
servings

220

25 mins

Caprese Zucchini Noodles

Ingredients:

- 4 medium zucchini (spiralized into noodles)
- 1 cup cherry tomatoes (halved)
- 8 oz fresh mozzarella balls (halved)
- 1/4 cup fresh basil leaves (chopped)
- 2 tbsp balsamic glaze
- 2 tbsp olive oil
- Salt and pepper to taste

Enjoy a lighter twist on the classic Caprese salad with zucchini noodles. Fresh zucchini noodles are tossed with cherry tomatoes, mozzarella, basil, and balsamic glaze for a refreshing and low-carb dish.

Directions

1. In a large skillet, heat olive oil over medium-high heat.
2. Add zucchini noodles and sauté for 3-4 mins until they are tender but still have a slight crunch.
3. Season with salt and pepper to taste.
4. In a large bowl, combine sautéed zucchini noodles, cherry tomatoes, halved fresh mozzarella balls, and chopped fresh basil.
5. Drizzle with balsamic glaze.
6. Toss gently to combine.
7. Serve immediately.
8. Enjoy!

Fun Facts

Zucchini noodles are a low-carb alternative to traditional pasta, perfect for a lighter meal.

4 servings

380 kcal

45 mins

Eggplant Parmesan

Ingredients:

- 2 large eggplants (sliced into 1/2-inch rounds)
- 2 cups marinara sauce
- 2 cups shredded mozzarella cheese
- 1 cup grated Parmesan cheese
- 2 cups breadcrumbs
- 2 eggs (beaten)
- 2 tsp dried Italian seasoning
- Olive oil for frying
- Salt and pepper to taste

Fun Facts

Eggplant Parmesan is a classic Italian-American comfort food that's both crispy and cheesy.

Indulge in the classic comfort of eggplant Parmesan. Slices of eggplant are breaded, fried to golden perfection, and layered with marinara sauce and melted mozzarella cheese for a hearty Italian dish.

Directions

1. Preheat the oven to 375°F (190°C).
2. Place eggplant slices in a colander, sprinkle with salt, and let them sit for 15 mins to release excess moisture. Pat them dry with paper towels.
3. In a shallow dish, mix breadcrumbs and dried Italian seasoning.
4. Dip eggplant slices in beaten eggs, then coat with breadcrumb mixture, pressing gently to adhere.
5. In a large skillet, heat olive oil over medium-high heat.
6. Fry eggplant slices in batches until golden brown and crispy, about 2-3 mins per side. Drain on paper towels.
7. In a baking dish, spread a thin layer of marinara sauce.
8. Place a layer of fried eggplant slices on top.
9. Top with shredded mozzarella and grated Parmesan cheese.
10. Repeat the layers until all ingredients are used, finishing with cheese on top.
11. Bake for 25-30 mins, or until cheese is melted and bubbly.
12. Serve hot.
13. Enjoy!

4
servings

320

45 mins

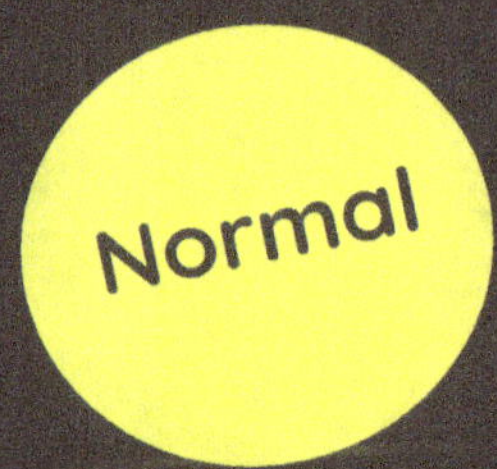

Broccoli Cheddar Stuffed Potatoes

Ingredients:

- 4 large russet potatoes
- 2 cups broccoli florets (steamed and chopped)
- 1.5 cups shredded cheddar cheese
- 1/2 cup sour cream
- 2 cloves garlic (minced)
- 2 tbsp butter
- 2 tbsp fresh chives (chopped)
- Salt and pepper to taste

Dive into the comforting goodness of broccoli cheddar stuffed potatoes. Baked potatoes are loaded with a creamy broccoli and cheddar cheese filling for a satisfying meal.

Directions

1. Preheat oven to 400°F (200°C).
2. Wash and scrub potatoes, then pierce them with a fork in several places.
3. Place potatoes on a baking sheet and bake for 45-50 mins, or until they are tender when pierced with a fork.
4. While the potatoes are baking, steam the broccoli florets until tender. Chop them into small pieces.
5. In a bowl, combine steamed broccoli, shredded cheddar cheese, minced garlic, sour cream, butter, and chopped fresh chives.
6. Season with salt and pepper to taste.
7. Once the potatoes are done, remove them from the oven.
8. Slice each potato open and fluff the flesh with a fork.
9. Stuff each potato with the broccoli and cheddar mixture.
10. Return the stuffed potatoes to the oven for 5-7 mins, or until the cheese is melted and bubbly.
11. Serve hot.
12. Enjoy!

Fun Facts

Stuffed potatoes are a hearty and comforting dish that can be customized with various fillings.

4 servings

260

35 mins

Teriyaki Glazed Portobello Mushrooms

Ingredients:

- 4 large Portobello mushrooms (stems removed)
- 1/2 cup teriyaki sauce
- 2 cloves garlic (minced)
- 2 tbsp vegetable oil
- 2 tbsp fresh parsley (chopped)
- 1 tsp sesame seeds (for garnish)
- Salt and pepper to taste

Fun Facts

Portobello mushrooms are a popular choice for vegetarian grilling, known for their meaty texture.

Enjoy the umami-rich flavors of teriyaki glazed Portobello mushrooms. Meaty Portobello mushrooms are marinated in a savory teriyaki sauce and grilled to perfection.

Directions

1. In a bowl, mix teriyaki sauce, minced garlic, and vegetable oil to make the marinade.
2. Season Portobello mushrooms with salt and pepper.
3. Place mushrooms in a shallow dish and pour the teriyaki marinade over them. Let them marinate for 15-20 mins, turning occasionally.
4. Preheat grill to medium-high heat.
5. Remove mushrooms from the marinade and grill for 4-5 mins per side, or until they are tender and have grill marks.
6. Brush with any remaining marinade during grilling.
7. Sprinkle with chopped fresh parsley and sesame seeds for garnish.
8. Serve hot.
9. Enjoy!

4 servings

160

20 mins

Cilantro Lime Corn on the Cob

Ingredients:

- 4 ears of fresh corn on the cob (husks and silk removed)
- 4 tbsp unsalted butter (softened)
- Zest and juice of 1 lime
- 2 tbsp fresh cilantro (chopped)
- Salt and pepper to taste

Brighten up your meal with cilantro lime corn on the cob. Fresh corn on the cob is grilled to perfection and brushed with a zesty cilantro lime butter for a burst of flavor.

Directions

1. Preheat grill to medium-high heat.
2. In a bowl, combine softened unsalted butter, lime zest, lime juice, chopped fresh cilantro, salt, and pepper.
3. Grill corn on the cob for 10-15 mins, turning occasionally, until they are tender and slightly charred.
4. Brush the cilantro lime butter mixture over the grilled corn.
5. Serve hot.
6. Enjoy!

Fun Facts

Grilled corn on the cob is a popular summer side dish, and the cilantro lime butter adds a fresh twist.

Chapter 7:
Pasta Pleasures

4
servings

320

20 mins

Garlic Parmesan Linguine

Ingredients:

- 8 oz linguine pasta
- 3 cloves garlic (minced)
- 2 tbsp unsalted butter
- 1 cup heavy cream
- 1 cup grated Parmesan cheese
- Salt and pepper to taste
- Fresh parsley (chopped, for garnish)

Fun Facts

Garlic Parmesan linguine is a classic Italian pasta dish known for its creamy and cheesy flavors.

Dive into the classic comfort of garlic Parmesan linguine. Cooked linguine pasta is tossed in a creamy garlic Parmesan sauce for a simple yet indulgent dish.

Directions

1. Cook linguine pasta according to package instructions until al dente. Drain and set aside.
2. In a skillet, melt unsalted butter over medium heat.
3. Add minced garlic and sauté for 1 min until fragrant.
4. Pour in heavy cream and bring to a simmer.
5. Reduce heat to low and stir in grated Parmesan cheese until the sauce is smooth and creamy.
6. Season with salt and pepper to taste.
7. Add cooked linguine to the skillet and toss to coat in the garlic Parmesan sauce.
8. Cook for an additional 2-3 mins until heated through.
9. Garnish with chopped fresh parsley.
10. Serve hot.
11. Enjoy!

4
servings

380

30 mins

Spinach and Artichoke Penne

Enjoy the creamy delight of spinach and artichoke penne. Penne pasta is coated in a rich spinach and artichoke cream sauce for a decadent and flavorful meal.

Ingredients:

- 8 oz penne pasta
- 8 oz fresh spinach (chopped)
- 1 can (14 oz) artichoke hearts (drained and chopped)
- 1 cup heavy cream
- 1/2 cup grated Parmesan cheese
- 2 cloves garlic (minced)
- 2 tbsp unsalted butter
- Salt and pepper to taste
- Red pepper flakes (optional, for heat)
- Fresh basil leaves (chopped, for garnish)

Directions

1. Cook penne pasta according to package instructions until al dente. Drain and set aside.
2. In a large skillet, melt unsalted butter over medium heat.
3. Add minced garlic and sauté for 1 min until fragrant.
4. Stir in chopped fresh spinach and sauté until wilted.
5. Add chopped artichoke hearts and cook for an additional 2-3 mins.
6. Pour in heavy cream and bring to a simmer.
7. Reduce heat to low and stir in grated Parmesan cheese until the sauce is creamy.
8. Season with salt, pepper, and red pepper flakes (if using) to taste.
9. Add cooked penne pasta to the skillet and toss to coat in the spinach and artichoke cream sauce.
10. Cook for an additional 2-3 mins until heated through.
11. Garnish with chopped fresh basil leaves.
12. Serve hot.
13. Enjoy!

Fun Facts

Spinach and artichoke pasta is a creamy and flavorful dish inspired by the popular dip.

4 servings   **360**   **25 mins**

Creamy Pesto Fusilli

Delight in the vibrant flavors of creamy pesto fusilli. Fusilli pasta is tossed in a luscious creamy pesto sauce for a satisfying and herbaceous dish.

Ingredients:

- 8 oz fusilli pasta
- 1/2 cup pesto sauce (store-bought or homemade)
- 1/2 cup heavy cream
- 1/4 cup grated Parmesan cheese
- 2 cloves garlic (minced)
- 2 tbsp unsalted butter
- Salt and pepper to taste
- Cherry tomatoes (halved, for garnish)
- Fresh basil leaves (chopped, for garnish)

Directions

1. Cook fusilli pasta according to package instructions until al dente. Drain and set aside.
2. In a skillet, melt unsalted butter over medium heat.
3. Add minced garlic and sauté for 1 min until fragrant.
4. Pour in heavy cream and bring to a simmer.
5. Reduce heat to low and stir in pesto sauce and grated Parmesan cheese until the sauce is creamy and well combined.
6. Season with salt and pepper to taste.
7. Add cooked fusilli pasta to the skillet and toss to coat in the creamy pesto sauce.
8. Cook for an additional 2-3 mins until heated through.
9. Garnish with halved cherry tomatoes and chopped fresh basil leaves.
10. Serve hot.
11. Enjoy!

Fun Facts

Creamy pesto fusilli is a delightful pasta dish that combines the richness of cream with the freshness of pesto.

4
servings

420

30 mins

Spaghetti Carbonara

Ingredients:

- 8 oz spaghetti
- 4 oz pancetta or guanciale (diced)
- 2 large eggs
- 1 cup grated Pecorino Romano cheese (or Parmesan)
- 2 cloves garlic (minced)
- Salt and black pepper to taste
- Fresh parsley (chopped, for garnish)

Fun Facts

Spaghetti carbonara is a beloved Roman pasta dish known for its creamy and savory sauce.

Savor the classic flavors of spaghetti carbonara. Spaghetti is tossed with a creamy sauce made from eggs, cheese, pancetta, and black pepper for an authentic Italian experience.

Directions

1. Cook spaghetti pasta according to package instructions until al dente. Drain and set aside, reserving 1/2 cup of pasta cooking water.
2. In a skillet, cook diced pancetta or guanciale over medium heat until it becomes crispy and golden brown. Remove from heat and set aside.
3. In a bowl, whisk together eggs, grated Pecorino Romano cheese (or Parmesan), minced garlic, and a generous amount of black pepper.
4. Quickly toss the cooked spaghetti with the crispy pancetta.
5. Pour the egg and cheese mixture over the hot pasta and toss vigorously to combine. The heat from the pasta will create a creamy sauce.
6. If the sauce is too thick, gradually add some of the reserved pasta cooking water to achieve the desired consistency.
7. Season with salt to taste.
8. Garnish with chopped fresh parsley.
9. Serve hot.
10. Enjoy!

4
servings

280

25 mins

Tomato Basil Orzo

Ingredients:

- 1 cup orzo pasta
- 1 can (14 oz) diced tomatoes
- 2 cloves garlic (minced)
- 1/4 cup fresh basil (chopped)
- 2 tbsp olive oil
- 1/4 cup grated Parmesan cheese
- Salt and pepper to taste
- Red pepper flakes (optional, for heat)
- Fresh basil leaves (for garnish)

Fun Facts

Tomato basil orzo is a simple yet flavorful pasta dish that celebrates the freshness of tomatoes and basil.

Brighten your meal with the flavors of tomato basil orzo. Tender orzo pasta is cooked in a vibrant tomato and basil sauce for a fresh and delightful side dish.

Directions

1. Cook orzo pasta according to package instructions until al dente. Drain and set aside.
2. In a skillet, heat olive oil over medium heat.
3. Add minced garlic and sauté for 1 min until fragrant.
4. Stir in diced tomatoes (with their juice) and chopped fresh basil.
5. Cook for 5-7 mins, allowing the sauce to simmer and thicken.
6. Season with salt, pepper, and red pepper flakes (if using) to taste.
7. Add cooked orzo pasta to the skillet and toss to coat in the tomato basil sauce.
8. Cook for an additional 2-3 mins until heated through.
9. Stir in grated Parmesan cheese until well combined.
10. Serve hot.
11. Garnish with fresh basil leaves.
12. Enjoy!

4
servings

350

30 mins

Lemon Garlic Shrimp Pasta

Ingredients:

- 8 oz linguine pasta
- 1 lb large shrimp (peeled and deveined)
- 3 cloves garlic (minced)
- 2 tbsp unsalted butter
- Zest and juice of 1 lemon
- 1/4 cup fresh parsley (chopped)
- Salt and black pepper to taste
- Red pepper flakes (optional, for heat)
- Grated Parmesan cheese (for garnish)

Fun Facts

Lemon garlic shrimp pasta is a zesty and vibrant dish that pairs perfectly with seafood.

Enjoy the zesty flavors of lemon garlic shrimp pasta. Succulent shrimp are sautéed in a lemon garlic butter sauce and served over linguine for a refreshing and satisfying dish.

Directions

1. Cook linguine pasta according to package instructions until al dente. Drain and set aside.
2. Season shrimp with salt, black pepper, and red pepper flakes (if using).
3. In a skillet, melt unsalted butter over medium-high heat.
4. Add minced garlic and sauté for 1 min until fragrant.
5. Add seasoned shrimp to the skillet and cook for 2-3 mins per side until they turn pink and opaque.
6. Stir in lemon zest, lemon juice, and chopped fresh parsley.
7. Toss cooked linguine with the lemon garlic butter sauce and shrimp.
8. Cook for an additional 2-3 mins to heat through.
9. Serve hot.
10. Garnish with grated Parmesan cheese.
11. Enjoy!

4 servings

450

35 mins

Creamy Bacon Ranch Mac and Cheese

Ingredients:

- 8 oz macaroni pasta
- 1 cup shredded cheddar cheese
- 1 cup shredded Monterey Jack cheese
- 1 cup milk
- 4 strips bacon (cooked and crumbled)
- 2 tbsp unsalted butter
- 1 packet ranch seasoning mix
- Salt and black pepper to taste
- Fresh chives (chopped, for garnish)

Fun Facts

Creamy bacon ranch mac and cheese is a flavorful twist on the classic comfort food.

Dive into the indulgence of creamy bacon ranch mac and cheese. Macaroni pasta is smothered in a luscious creamy cheese sauce, then topped with crispy bacon and ranch seasoning for a satisfying meal.

Directions

1. Cook macaroni pasta according to package instructions until al dente. Drain and set aside.
2. In a saucepan, melt unsalted butter over medium heat.
3. Stir in shredded cheddar cheese and shredded Monterey Jack cheese until melted and smooth.
4. Gradually pour in milk, stirring continuously until the sauce is creamy.
5. Season with ranch seasoning mix, salt, and black pepper to taste.
6. Add cooked macaroni pasta to the sauce and toss to coat.
7. Cook for an additional 2-3 mins to heat through.
8. Stir in crumbled bacon.
9. Serve hot.
10. Garnish with chopped fresh chives.
11. Enjoy!

4
servings

390

35 mins

Penne Alla Vodka

Indulge in the creamy elegance of penne alla vodka. Penne pasta is coated in a velvety tomato vodka sauce, creating a luxurious and comforting Italian dish.

Ingredients:

- 8 oz penne pasta
- 1 can (14 oz) crushed tomatoes
- 1/2 cup heavy cream
- 1/4 cup vodka
- 2 cloves garlic (minced)
- 2 tbsp unsalted butter
- 2 tbsp olive oil
- 1/4 cup grated Parmesan cheese
- Salt and black pepper to taste
- Fresh basil leaves (chopped, for garnish)

Directions

1. Cook penne pasta according to package instructions until al dente. Drain and set aside.
2. In a large skillet, heat olive oil and unsalted butter over medium heat.
3. Add minced garlic and sauté for 1 min until fragrant.
4. Pour in vodka and cook for 2-3 mins to reduce slightly.
5. Stir in crushed tomatoes and heavy cream.
6. Simmer for 10-15 mins, allowing the sauce to thicken.
7. Season with salt and black pepper to taste.
8. Add cooked penne pasta to the skillet and toss to coat in the tomato vodka sauce.
9. Cook for an additional 2-3 mins until heated through.
10. Stir in grated Parmesan cheese.
11. Garnish with chopped fresh basil leaves.
12. Serve hot.
13. Enjoy!

Fun Facts

Penne alla vodka is a rich and creamy pasta dish with a touch of elegance from the vodka.

4 servings

340

30 mins

Garlic Butter Mushroom Fettuccine

Ingredients:

- 8 oz fettuccine pasta
- 8 oz mushrooms (sliced)
- 3 cloves garlic (minced)
- 2 tbsp unsalted butter
- 2 tbsp olive oil
- 1/4 cup heavy cream
- 1/4 cup grated Parmesan cheese
- Salt and black pepper to taste
- Fresh parsley (chopped, for garnish)

Fun Facts

Garlic butter mushroom fettuccine is a savory pasta dish with the earthy goodness of mushrooms.

Dive into the earthy flavors of garlic butter mushroom fettuccine. Fettuccine pasta is coated in a velvety garlic butter sauce with sautéed mushrooms for a comforting and savory meal.

Directions

1. Cook fettuccine pasta according to package instructions until al dente. Drain and set aside.
2. In a large skillet, heat olive oil and unsalted butter over medium heat.
3. Add minced garlic and sliced mushrooms.
4. Sauté until mushrooms are tender and browned, about 5-7 mins.
5. Pour in heavy cream and simmer for 2-3 mins.
6. Stir in grated Parmesan cheese until the sauce is creamy.
7. Season with salt and black pepper to taste.
8. Add cooked fettuccine pasta to the skillet and toss to coat in the garlic butter mushroom sauce.
9. Cook for an additional 2-3 mins until heated through.
10. Garnish with chopped fresh parsley.
11. Serve hot.
12. Enjoy!

4
servings

480

40 mins

Beef Stroganoff with Rotini

Indulge in the hearty flavors of beef stroganoff with rotini. Tender strips of beef are cooked in a creamy mushroom sauce and served over rotini pasta for a comforting and satisfying meal.

Ingredients:

- 8 oz rotini pasta
- 1 lb beef sirloin or tenderloin (thinly sliced)
- 8 oz mushrooms (sliced)
- 1 onion (chopped)
- 3 cloves garlic (minced)
- 1 cup beef broth
- 1/2 cup sour cream
- 2 tbsp olive oil
- 2 tbsp all-purpose flour
- 2 tsp Worcestershire sauce
- 2 tsp Dijon mustard
- Salt and black pepper to taste
- Fresh parsley (chopped, for garnish)

Directions

1. Cook rotini pasta according to package instructions until al dente. Drain and set aside.
2. In a large skillet, heat olive oil over medium-high heat.
3. Add thinly sliced beef and cook for 2-3 mins until browned. Remove beef from the skillet and set aside.
4. In the same skillet, add chopped onions and sliced mushrooms. Sauté until mushrooms are tender and onions are translucent, about 5-7 mins.
5. Stir in minced garlic and cook for 1 min until fragrant.
6. Sprinkle all-purpose flour over the mushroom mixture and stir to combine. Cook for 1-2 mins.
7. Gradually pour in beef broth, Worcestershire sauce, and Dijon mustard, stirring constantly until the sauce thickens.
8. Return the cooked beef to the skillet and simmer for 5 mins, allowing the flavors to meld.
9. Season with salt and black pepper to taste.
10. Stir in sour cream until the sauce is creamy.
11. Add cooked rotini pasta to the skillet and toss to coat in the beef stroganoff sauce.
12. Cook for an additional 2-3 mins until heated through.
13. Garnish with chopped fresh parsley.
14. Serve hot.
15. Enjoy!

Fun Facts

Beef stroganoff with rotini is a hearty and comforting pasta dish that's perfect for a satisfying meal.

Chapter 8:
Sensational Sides

4
servings

180

30 mins

Roasted Brussels Sprouts with Balsamic Glaze

Elevate your meal with the irresistible flavors of roasted Brussels sprouts with balsamic glaze. Brussels sprouts are roasted to perfection and drizzled with a sweet and tangy balsamic glaze for a sensational side dish.

Ingredients:

- 1 lb Brussels sprouts (trimmed and halved)
- 2 tbsp olive oil
- Salt and black pepper to taste
- 2 tbsp balsamic vinegar
- 1 tbsp honey
- 2 cloves garlic (minced)
- Fresh parsley (chopped, for garnish)

Directions

1. Preheat oven to 425°F (218°C).
2. In a bowl, toss halved Brussels sprouts with olive oil, salt, and black pepper to coat evenly.
3. Spread Brussels sprouts in a single layer on a baking sheet lined with parchment paper.
4. Roast for 20-25 mins, or until Brussels sprouts are tender and caramelized, stirring halfway through.
5. In a small saucepan, combine balsamic vinegar, honey, and minced garlic.
6. Simmer over low heat for 5-7 mins, or until the glaze thickens.
7. Drizzle the balsamic glaze over the roasted Brussels sprouts.
8. Garnish with chopped fresh parsley.
9. Serve hot.
10. Enjoy!

Fun Facts

Roasted Brussels sprouts with balsamic glaze offer a perfect balance of sweet and tangy flavors.

4
servings

280

35 mins

Garlic Mashed Potatoes

Ingredients:

- 4 large russet potatoes (peeled and diced)
- 4 cloves garlic (minced)
- 1/2 cup heavy cream
- 2 tbsp unsalted butter
- Salt and black pepper to taste
- Fresh chives (chopped, for garnish)
- Grated Parmesan cheese (optional, for garnish)

Fun Facts

Garlic mashed potatoes are a classic comfort food side dish with a flavorful twist from the garlic.

Savor the creamy goodness of garlic mashed potatoes. Russet potatoes are boiled until tender, mashed with garlic-infused cream, and seasoned to perfection for a classic side dish that complements any meal.

Directions

1. Place diced russet potatoes in a large pot and cover with cold water.
2. Bring the water to a boil over high heat and cook until potatoes are fork-tender, about 15-20 mins.
3. While the potatoes are boiling, combine minced garlic and heavy cream in a saucepan over low heat. Heat until the cream is warm, then remove from heat and let the garlic infuse the cream.
4. Drain the cooked potatoes and return them to the pot.
5. Mash the potatoes with a potato masher or a hand mixer until smooth.
6. Gradually pour in the garlic-infused cream and mix until the mashed potatoes are creamy.
7. Stir in unsalted butter until melted and fully incorporated.
8. Season with salt and black pepper to taste.
9. Garnish with chopped fresh chives and grated Parmesan cheese (if desired).
10. Serve hot.
11. Enjoy!

4
servings

120

20 mins

Lemon Butter Asparagus

Ingredients:

- 1 lb fresh asparagus spears (trimmed)
- 2 tbsp unsalted butter
- Zest and juice of 1 lemon
- Salt and black pepper to taste
- Fresh parsley (chopped, for garnish)

Brighten up your meal with lemon butter asparagus. Fresh asparagus spears are sautéed in a lemon butter sauce for a vibrant and tender side dish that pairs perfectly with any entrée.

Directions

1. In a large skillet, melt unsalted butter over medium-high heat.
2. Add trimmed asparagus spears to the skillet and sauté for 5-7 mins, or until they are tender and bright green.
3. Stir in lemon zest and lemon juice, tossing to coat the asparagus evenly.
4. Season with salt and black pepper to taste.
5. Cook for an additional 1-2 mins to heat through.
6. Garnish with chopped fresh parsley.
7. Serve hot.
8. Enjoy!

Fun Facts

Lemon butter asparagus is a refreshing and zesty side dish that adds brightness to your plate.

4 servings | **160** kcal | **25 mins**

Parmesan Roasted Cauliflower

Ingredients:

- 1 head cauliflower (cut into florets)
- 1/4 cup grated Parmesan cheese
- 2 tbsp olive oil
- 1 tsp garlic powder
- 1 tsp dried thyme
- Salt and black pepper to taste
- Fresh parsley (chopped, for garnish)

Delight in the savory flavors of Parmesan roasted cauliflower. Cauliflower florets are roasted with Parmesan cheese and herbs until golden and crispy for a satisfying and nutritious side dish.

Directions

1. Preheat oven to 425°F (218°C).
2. In a large bowl, toss cauliflower florets with olive oil, grated Parmesan cheese, garlic powder, dried thyme, salt, and black pepper to coat evenly.
3. Spread cauliflower in a single layer on a baking sheet lined with parchment paper.
4. Roast for 20-25 mins, or until cauliflower is tender and golden brown, stirring halfway through.
5. Garnish with chopped fresh parsley.
6. Serve hot.
7. Enjoy!

Fun Facts

Parmesan roasted cauliflower is a crispy and cheesy side dish that's packed with flavor.

**4
servings**

140

25 mins

Honey Glazed Carrots

Ingredients:

- 1 lb carrots (peeled and sliced into coins)
- 2 tbsp unsalted butter
- 2 tbsp honey
- Salt and black pepper to taste
- Fresh parsley (chopped, for garnish)

Enjoy the sweet and savory goodness of honey glazed carrots. Carrot coins are sautéed in a honey-butter glaze until tender and caramelized for a delightful side dish.

Directions

1. In a large skillet, melt unsalted butter over medium-high heat.
2. Add carrot coins to the skillet and sauté for 5-7 mins, or until they start to become tender.
3. Stir in honey and continue to cook for an additional 10-12 mins, or until carrots are tender and caramelized, stirring occasionally.
4. Season with salt and black pepper to taste.
5. Garnish with chopped fresh parsley.
6. Serve hot.
7. Enjoy!

Fun Facts

Honey glazed carrots are a simple yet flavorful side dish that adds sweetness to your meal.

4
servings

220

30 mins

Creamed Spinach

Dive into the velvety richness of creamed spinach. Fresh spinach is sautéed in a creamy garlic sauce and seasoned to perfection for a decadent and comforting side dish.

Ingredients:

- 1 lb fresh spinach (chopped)
- 1/2 cup heavy cream
- 2 cloves garlic (minced)
- 2 tbsp unsalted butter
- 1/4 cup grated Parmesan cheese
- Salt and black pepper to taste
- Nutmeg (optional, for a pinch of warmth)
- Grated nutmeg (for garnish, optional)

Directions

1. In a large skillet, melt unsalted butter over medium heat.
2. Add minced garlic and sauté for 1 min until fragrant.
3. Stir in chopped fresh spinach and sauté until wilted.
4. Pour in heavy cream and bring to a simmer.
5. Cook for 10-15 mins, or until the creamed spinach thickens and the spinach is tender.
6. Stir in grated Parmesan cheese until the sauce is creamy.
7. Season with salt and black pepper to taste. Add a pinch of nutmeg for warmth if desired.
8. Cook for an additional 2-3 mins.
9. Garnish with grated nutmeg (if desired).
10. Serve hot.
11. Enjoy!

Fun Facts

Creamed spinach is a rich and comforting side dish that pairs beautifully with various entrees.

4
servings

180

30 mins

Baked Sweet Potato Wedges

Ingredients:

- 2 large sweet potatoes (cut into wedges)
- 2 tbsp olive oil
- 1 tsp paprika
- 1 tsp dried rosemary
- 1 tsp garlic powder
- Salt and black pepper to taste
- Fresh parsley (chopped, for garnish)

Fun Facts

Baked sweet potato wedges are a healthier alternative to traditional fries, packed with flavor.

Satisfy your craving for sweet and savory with baked sweet potato wedges. Sweet potato wedges are seasoned with herbs and baked to perfection for a wholesome and delicious side dish.

Directions

1. Preheat oven to 425°F (218°C).
2. In a large bowl, toss sweet potato wedges with olive oil, paprika, dried rosemary, garlic powder, salt, and black pepper to coat evenly.
3. Spread sweet potato wedges in a single layer on a baking sheet lined with parchment paper.
4. Bake for 25-30 mins, or until sweet potato wedges are tender and crispy, flipping halfway through.
5. Garnish with chopped fresh parsley.
6. Serve hot.
7. Enjoy!

4 servings

220

20 mins

Cilantro Lime Rice

Ingredients:

- 1 cup long-grain white rice
- Zest and juice of 2 limes
- 2 tbsp fresh cilantro (chopped)
- 1 clove garlic (minced)
- 2 cups water
- Salt to taste
- Fresh cilantro leaves (for garnish)

Brighten your plate with cilantro lime rice. Long-grain rice is cooked with zesty lime juice and fresh cilantro for a fragrant and vibrant side dish that complements a variety of cuisines.

Directions

1. Rinse the long-grain white rice under cold water until the water runs clear. Drain.
2. In a saucepan, combine rinsed rice, water, minced garlic, and salt.
3. Bring to a boil over high heat, then reduce heat to low, cover, and simmer for 15-18 mins, or until the rice is tender and the liquid is absorbed.
4. Fluff the cooked rice with a fork.
5. Stir in lime zest, lime juice, and chopped fresh cilantro.
6. Garnish with fresh cilantro leaves.
7. Serve hot.
8. Enjoy!

Fun Facts

Cilantro lime rice is a refreshing and fragrant side dish that pairs perfectly with Mexican cuisine.

4 servings | **140** kcal | **25 mins**

Garlic Butter Mushrooms

Ingredients:

- 1 lb button mushrooms (sliced)
- 2 cloves garlic (minced)
- 2 tbsp unsalted butter
- 1 tbsp olive oil
- 2 tbsp fresh parsley (chopped)
- Salt and black pepper to taste
- Grated Parmesan cheese (for garnish, optional)

Fun Facts

Garlic butter mushrooms are a savory and aromatic side dish that complements various meals.

Delight in the earthy flavors of garlic butter mushrooms. Button mushrooms are sautéed in a savory garlic butter sauce and seasoned to perfection for a savory and aromatic side dish.

Directions

1. In a large skillet, heat olive oil and unsalted butter over medium-high heat.
2. Add sliced button mushrooms to the skillet and sauté for 5-7 mins, or until they are tender and browned.
3. Stir in minced garlic and cook for 1 min until fragrant.
4. Season with salt and black pepper to taste.
5. Cook for an additional 2-3 mins.
6. Garnish with chopped fresh parsley and grated Parmesan cheese (if desired).
7. Serve hot.
8. Enjoy!

4
servings

320

40 mins

Cheesy Broccoli Casserole

Ingredients:

- 1 lb fresh broccoli florets
- 1 cup shredded cheddar cheese
- 1/2 cup mayonnaise
- 1/2 cup sour cream
- 1/4 cup grated Parmesan cheese
- 2 cloves garlic (minced)
- 1/2 cup breadcrumbs
- 2 tbsp unsalted butter (melted)
- Salt and black pepper to taste
- Fresh parsley (chopped, for garnish)

Fun Facts

Cheesy broccoli casserole is a comforting and cheesy side dish that's perfect for gatherings.

Dive into the creamy indulgence of cheesy broccoli casserole. Tender broccoli florets are baked in a cheesy sauce and topped with a crispy breadcrumb topping for a comforting and irresistible side dish.

Directions

1. Preheat oven to 350°F (175°C).
2. Steam or blanch broccoli florets until they are tender-crisp, about 3-5 mins. Drain and set aside.
3. In a bowl, combine shredded cheddar cheese, mayonnaise, sour cream, grated Parmesan cheese, and minced garlic.
4. Season with salt and black pepper to taste.
5. Place steamed broccoli in a baking dish and spread the cheese mixture over the top.
6. In a separate bowl, combine breadcrumbs and melted unsalted butter.
7. Sprinkle the breadcrumb mixture evenly over the cheese mixture.
8. Bake for 20-25 mins, or until the casserole is bubbly and the breadcrumb topping is golden brown.
9. Garnish with chopped fresh parsley.
10. Serve hot.
11. Enjoy!

Chapter 9:
International Inspirations

4
servings

380

40 mins

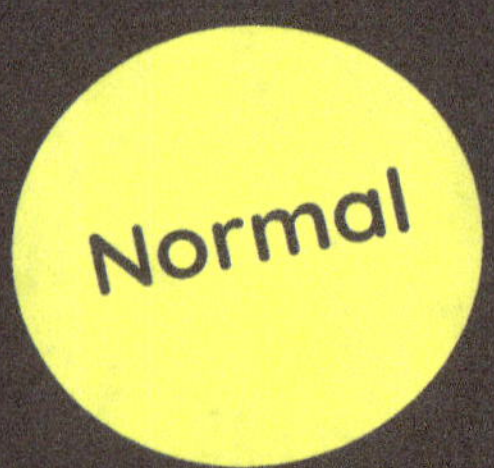

Thai Red Curry Chicken

Ingredients:

- 1 lb boneless chicken thighs (cut into bite-sized pieces)
- 1 can (14 oz) coconut milk
- 2-3 tbsp red curry paste
- 1 red bell pepper (sliced)
- 1 onion (sliced)
- 1 zucchini (sliced)
- 2 cloves garlic (minced)
- 1 tsp fresh ginger (minced)
- 2 tbsp vegetable oil
- 1 tbsp fish sauce
- 1 tbsp brown sugar
- Fresh cilantro leaves (for garnish)
- Lime wedges (for garnish)
- Cooked jasmine rice (for serving)

Fun Facts

Thai red curry chicken is a flavorful and exotic dish that captures the essence of Thai cuisine.

Embark on a flavor journey with Thai red curry chicken. Tender chicken is simmered in a rich and aromatic red curry sauce, infused with coconut milk and Thai spices, for a delectable and exotic dish.

Directions

1. Heat vegetable oil in a large skillet or wok over medium-high heat.
2. Add minced garlic and minced ginger to the skillet. Sauté for 1 min until fragrant.
3. Stir in red curry paste and cook for 1-2 mins until fragrant.
4. Add chicken pieces and cook until they are browned on all sides.
5. Add sliced red bell pepper, sliced onion, and sliced zucchini to the skillet. Sauté for 3-5 mins until vegetables are slightly tender.
6. Pour in coconut milk, fish sauce, and brown sugar. Stir to combine.
7. Simmer for 15-20 mins, or until the chicken is cooked through and the sauce thickens.
8. Season with additional fish sauce or brown sugar to taste, if desired.
9. Serve Thai red curry chicken over cooked jasmine rice.
10. Garnish with fresh cilantro leaves and lime wedges.
11. Enjoy!

4 servings | **340** | **30 mins**

Beef and Broccoli Stir-Fry

Ingredients:

- 1 lb flank steak (sliced into thin strips)
- 1 lb broccoli florets
- 2 cloves garlic (minced)
- 1/4 cup soy sauce
- 2 tbsp oyster sauce
- 1 tbsp brown sugar
- 1 tsp sesame oil
- 1 tsp cornstarch
- 2 tbsp vegetable oil
- Sesame seeds (for garnish, optional)
- Cooked white rice (for serving)

Fun Facts

Beef and broccoli stir-fry is a classic Chinese dish that's quick and full of flavor.

Savor the savory delights of beef and broccoli stir-fry. Tender slices of beef are stir-fried with crisp broccoli florets in a savory brown sauce for a quick and delicious Chinese-inspired dish.

Directions

1. In a bowl, whisk together soy sauce, oyster sauce, brown sugar, sesame oil, and cornstarch. Set aside.
2. Heat vegetable oil in a large skillet or wok over high heat.
3. Add minced garlic and sliced beef to the skillet. Stir-fry for 2-3 mins until beef is browned.
4. Remove the beef from the skillet and set aside.
5. Add broccoli florets to the skillet and stir-fry for 3-5 mins until they are tender-crisp.
6. Return the cooked beef to the skillet.
7. Pour the sauce mixture over the beef and broccoli.
8. Stir-fry for an additional 2-3 mins, or until the sauce thickens and coats the beef and broccoli.
9. Serve beef and broccoli stir-fry over cooked white rice.
10. Garnish with sesame seeds if desired.
11. Enjoy!

4 servings   320   35 mins

Italian Caprese Chicken

Ingredients:

- 4 boneless chicken breasts
- 2 large tomatoes (sliced)
- 4 slices fresh mozzarella cheese
- Fresh basil leaves (for garnish)
- Balsamic glaze (for drizzling)
- Salt and black pepper to taste
- Olive oil (for drizzling)
- Fresh basil pesto (optional, for extra flavor)
- Cooked pasta or rice (for serving, optional)

Fun Facts

Italian Caprese chicken is a delightful and visually appealing dish inspired by the flavors of Italy.

Transport your taste buds to Italy with Italian Caprese chicken. Tender chicken breasts are topped with ripe tomatoes, fresh basil, and mozzarella cheese, then baked to perfection for a delightful Italian-inspired dish.

Directions

1. Preheat oven to 375°F (190°C).
2. Season chicken breasts with salt and black pepper to taste.
3. Heat olive oil in an ovenproof skillet over medium-high heat.
4. Add chicken breasts to the skillet and sear for 2-3 mins per side until browned.
5. Remove the chicken from the skillet and set aside.
6. In the same skillet, layer sliced tomatoes, fresh mozzarella cheese, and fresh basil leaves on top of each chicken breast.
7. Drizzle with olive oil and season with additional salt and black pepper if desired.
8. Bake in the preheated oven for 15-20 mins, or until the chicken is cooked through and the cheese is melted and bubbly.
9. Garnish with fresh basil leaves and drizzle with balsamic glaze (and basil pesto if desired).
10. Serve Italian Caprese chicken over cooked pasta or rice if desired.
11. Enjoy!

4
servings

480

40 mins

Tandoori Grilled Lamb Chops

Ingredients:

- 8 lamb chops
- 1 cup plain yogurt
- 2 tbsp tandoori spice blend
- 2 cloves garlic (minced)
- 1 tsp fresh ginger (minced)
- Juice of 1 lemon
- Salt and black pepper to taste
- Fresh cilantro leaves (for garnish)
- Lemon wedges (for garnish)
- Naan bread or rice (for serving)

Fun Facts

Tandoori grilled lamb chops are a flavorful and aromatic Indian-inspired dish that's perfect for grilling.

Indulge in the aromatic spices of tandoori grilled lamb chops. Tender lamb chops are marinated in a flavorful blend of yogurt and spices, then grilled to perfection for an Indian-inspired dish that's bursting with flavor.

Directions

1. In a bowl, whisk together plain yogurt, tandoori spice blend, minced garlic, minced fresh ginger, lemon juice, salt, and black pepper.
2. Place lamb chops in a resealable plastic bag or shallow dish.
3. Pour the yogurt marinade over the lamb chops and massage to coat evenly.
4. Seal the bag or cover the dish and refrigerate for at least 2 hours, or overnight for maximum flavor.
5. Preheat grill to medium-high heat.
6. Remove lamb chops from the marinade and grill for 3-4 mins per side, or to your desired level of doneness.
7. Garnish with fresh cilantro leaves and lemon wedges.
8. Serve tandoori grilled lamb chops with naan bread or rice.
9. Enjoy!

4
servings

380

30 mins

Shrimp Scampi Linguine

Ingredients:

- 8 oz linguine pasta
- 1 lb large shrimp (peeled and deveined)
- 4 cloves garlic (minced)
- 1/4 cup white wine
- 1/4 cup unsalted butter
- Juice of 1 lemon
- Red pepper flakes (optional, for heat)
- Salt and black pepper to taste
- Fresh parsley (chopped, for garnish)
- Grated Parmesan cheese (for garnish, optional)
- Lemon wedges (for garnish)

Fun Facts

Shrimp scampi linguine is a classic Italian dish with succulent shrimp in a garlic butter sauce.

Dive into the flavors of the sea with shrimp scampi linguine. Succulent shrimp are sautéed in a garlic-infused white wine and butter sauce, then tossed with linguine pasta for an indulgent Italian-inspired dish.

Directions

1. Cook linguine pasta according to package instructions until al dente. Drain and set aside.
2. In a large skillet, melt unsalted butter over medium heat.
3. Add minced garlic and red pepper flakes (if desired). Sauté for 1 min until fragrant.
4. Add peeled and deveined shrimp to the skillet and sauté for 2-3 mins until they turn pink.
5. Pour in white wine and lemon juice. Simmer for 2-3 mins.
6. Season with salt and black pepper to taste.
7. Toss cooked linguine pasta with the shrimp and sauce.
8. Garnish with chopped fresh parsley and grated Parmesan cheese (if desired).
9. Serve with lemon wedges.
10. Enjoy!

4
servings

280

40 mins

Greek Lemon Potatoes

Ingredients:

- 4 large russet potatoes (cut into wedges)
- 4 cloves garlic (minced)
- Zest and juice of 2 lemons
- 1/4 cup olive oil
- 1 tsp dried oregano
- 1 tsp dried thyme
- Salt and black pepper to taste
- Fresh parsley (chopped, for garnish)
- Lemon wedges (for garnish)
- Tzatziki sauce (for dipping, optional)

Fun Facts

Greek lemon potatoes are a zesty and flavorful side dish that pairs perfectly with Greek cuisine.

Enjoy the zesty goodness of Greek lemon potatoes. Potato wedges are roasted with a lemony garlic and herb marinade until crispy and infused with Mediterranean flavors for a delightful Greek-inspired side dish.

Directions

1. Preheat oven to 425°F (218°C).
2. In a bowl, whisk together minced garlic, lemon zest, lemon juice, olive oil, dried oregano, dried thyme, salt, and black pepper.
3. Toss potato wedges with the lemon marinade to coat evenly.
4. Spread potato wedges in a single layer on a baking sheet lined with parchment paper.
5. Roast for 30-35 mins, or until potatoes are crispy and golden brown, flipping halfway through.
6. Garnish with chopped fresh parsley and lemon wedges.
7. Serve Greek lemon potatoes with tzatziki sauce for dipping if desired.
8. Enjoy!

4 servings · **280** kcal · **30 mins**

Mexican Street Corn

Ingredients:

- 4 ears of corn (husked)
- 1/4 cup mayonnaise
- 1/4 cup sour cream
- 1/2 cup crumbled cotija cheese (or feta cheese)
- 1/2 tsp chili powder (adjust to taste)
- 1/4 cup fresh cilantro leaves (chopped)
- 1 lime (cut into wedges)
- Salt and black pepper to taste
- Hot sauce (optional, for heat)

Fun Facts

Mexican street corn, known as "elote," is a popular and flavorful street food in Mexico.

Delight in the bold flavors of Mexican street corn. Grilled corn on the cob is slathered with a creamy and tangy mayo-based sauce, then sprinkled with cheese and chili powder for a delicious Mexican-inspired treat.

Directions

1. Preheat grill to medium-high heat.
2. Grill corn on the cob for 10-15 mins, turning occasionally, until the corn is charred and tender.
3. In a bowl, combine mayonnaise, sour cream, crumbled cotija cheese, and chili powder. Mix well.
4. Season with salt and black pepper to taste. Add hot sauce for extra heat if desired.
5. Slather the grilled corn with the mayo-based sauce.
6. Sprinkle with chopped fresh cilantro leaves.
7. Serve Mexican street corn with lime wedges for squeezing over the top.
8. Enjoy!

4
servings

420

45 mins

Chicken Tikka Masala

Ingredients:

- 1 lb boneless chicken breasts (cut into bite-sized pieces)
- 1 cup plain yogurt
- 2 cloves garlic (minced)
- 1 tsp fresh ginger (minced)
- 2 tbsp garam masala
- 1 tsp paprika
- 1/2 tsp ground turmeric
- Salt and black pepper to taste
- 2 tbsp vegetable oil
- 1 onion (finely chopped)
- 1 can (14 oz) tomato sauce
- 1/2 cup heavy cream
- Fresh cilantro leaves (for garnish)
- Cooked basmati rice (for serving)

Fun Facts

Chicken tikka masala is a beloved and flavorful Indian dish with tender chicken in a creamy tomato sauce.

Indulge in the rich and aromatic flavors of chicken tikka masala. Tender chicken pieces are marinated in yogurt and spices, then simmered in a creamy tomato sauce for a delightful Indian-inspired dish.

Directions

1. In a bowl, combine plain yogurt, minced garlic, minced fresh ginger, garam masala, paprika, ground turmeric, salt, and black pepper.
2. Add chicken pieces to the marinade and toss to coat. Refrigerate for at least 1 hour, or overnight for maximum flavor.
3. Heat vegetable oil in a large skillet over medium-high heat.
4. Add finely chopped onion and sauté until translucent.
5. Add marinated chicken pieces and cook until they are browned on all sides.
6. Pour in tomato sauce and heavy cream. Simmer for 15-20 mins, or until the chicken is cooked through and the sauce thickens.
7. Season with additional salt and black pepper to taste, if desired.
8. Serve chicken tikka masala over cooked basmati rice.
9. Garnish with fresh cilantro leaves.
10. Enjoy!

4 servings

360 kcal

35 mins

Korean BBQ Beef

Ingredients:

- 1 lb thinly sliced beef (ribeye or flank steak)
- 1/4 cup soy sauce
- 2 tbsp brown sugar
- 2 cloves garlic (minced)
- 1 tsp fresh ginger (minced)
- 2 green onions (chopped)
- 1 tsp sesame oil
- 1 tsp toasted sesame seeds (for garnish)
- Cooked white rice (for serving)
- Kimchi (for serving, optional)

Fun Facts

Korean BBQ beef is a savory and sweet dish that's perfect for grilling and enjoying with rice.

Enjoy the savory and sweet flavors of Korean BBQ beef. Thinly sliced beef is marinated in a blend of soy sauce, garlic, and brown sugar, then grilled to perfection for a delicious Korean-inspired dish.

Directions

1. In a bowl, whisk together soy sauce, brown sugar, minced garlic, minced fresh ginger, chopped green onions, and sesame oil.
2. Add thinly sliced beef to the marinade and toss to coat. Refrigerate for at least 30 mins, or longer for extra flavor.
3. Preheat grill to high heat.
4. Grill marinated beef slices for 2-3 mins per side, or until they are cooked to your desired level of doneness.
5. Sprinkle with toasted sesame seeds for garnish.
6. Serve Korean BBQ beef over cooked white rice.
7. Enjoy! Optional: Serve with kimchi for added flavor.
8. Enjoy!

4
servings

320

30 mins

Spicy Thai Shrimp Soup

Ingredients:

- 1 lb large shrimp (peeled and deveined)
- 1 can (14 oz) coconut milk
- 2 cups chicken broth
- 2 stalks lemongrass (cut into 2-inch pieces)
- 2 slices galangal (or ginger)
- 2-3 red bird's eye chilies (adjust to taste)
- 3-4 kaffir lime leaves
- 2-3 cloves garlic (minced)
- 1 tsp fish sauce
- 1 tsp sugar
- Lime wedges (for garnish)
- Fresh cilantro leaves (for garnish)
- Thai basil leaves (for garnish)
- Thai bird's eye chilies (for garnish, optional)
- Cooked rice (for serving)

Fun Facts

Spicy Thai shrimp soup is a fragrant and invigorating dish that's bursting with Thai flavors.

Warm your soul with the bold and spicy flavors of Thai shrimp soup. Succulent shrimp are simmered in a spicy coconut milk broth with lemongrass, ginger, and Thai herbs for an invigorating Thai-inspired dish.

Directions

1. In a large pot, combine chicken broth, lemongrass, galangal or ginger, red bird's eye chilies, and kaffir lime leaves.
2. Bring to a simmer and let it cook for 10-15 mins to infuse the flavors.
3. Remove the aromatics from the broth.
4. Return the broth to a simmer and add minced garlic, coconut milk, and sugar. Stir to combine.
5. Add peeled and deveined shrimp to the simmering broth and cook for 2-3 mins until they turn pink.
6. Season with fish sauce to taste.
7. Serve spicy Thai shrimp soup over cooked rice.
8. Garnish with lime wedges, fresh cilantro leaves, Thai basil leaves, and Thai bird's eye chilies if desired.
9. Enjoy!

Chapter 10:
Vegetarian Voyages

4 servings

220

30 mins

Spinach and Feta Stuffed Portobello Mushrooms

Ingredients:

- 4 large portobello mushroom caps
- 2 cups fresh spinach (chopped)
- 1/2 cup crumbled feta cheese
- 2 cloves garlic (minced)
- 2 tbsp olive oil
- 1 tsp dried oregano
- Salt and black pepper to taste
- Fresh parsley (chopped, for garnish)
- Lemon wedges (for garnish)

Delight in the savory goodness of spinach and feta stuffed portobello mushrooms. Large portobello mushroom caps are filled with a flavorful mixture of spinach, feta cheese, and herbs, then baked to perfection for a vegetarian voyage of flavors.

Directions

1. Preheat oven to 375°F (190°C).
2. Remove the stems and gills from the portobello mushroom caps and brush them with olive oil on both sides.
3. In a skillet, heat olive oil over medium heat.
4. Add minced garlic and chopped fresh spinach. Sauté for 2-3 mins until spinach is wilted.
5. Remove from heat and stir in crumbled feta cheese, dried oregano, salt, and black pepper.
6. Fill each mushroom cap with the spinach and feta mixture.
7. Place the stuffed mushrooms on a baking sheet and bake for 15-20 mins, or until mushrooms are tender.
8. Garnish with chopped fresh parsley and serve with lemon wedges.
9. Enjoy!

Fun Facts

Spinach and feta stuffed portobello mushrooms are a delightful and savory vegetarian dish.

4 servings

320

20 mins

Caprese Stuffed Avocado

Ingredients:

- 2 ripe avocados (halved and pitted)
- 1 cup cherry tomatoes (halved)
- 1/2 cup fresh mozzarella balls (or cubed mozzarella)
- Fresh basil leaves (chopped)
- Balsamic glaze (for drizzling)
- Extra virgin olive oil (for drizzling)
- Salt and black pepper to taste
- Fresh basil leaves (for garnish)

Fun Facts

Caprese stuffed avocado is a fresh and healthy vegetarian dish that's perfect for a light meal.

Savor the fresh and creamy flavors of caprese stuffed avocado. Ripe avocados are filled with a delightful mixture of cherry tomatoes, mozzarella, basil, and balsamic glaze for a delicious and healthy vegetarian voyage.

Directions

1. Scoop out a little bit of the flesh from each avocado half to create a hollow space for stuffing.
2. In a bowl, combine cherry tomatoes, fresh mozzarella, and chopped fresh basil.
3. Drizzle with extra virgin olive oil and season with salt and black pepper to taste. Toss to combine.
4. Spoon the tomato and mozzarella mixture into the hollowed-out avocado halves.
5. Drizzle with balsamic glaze and garnish with additional fresh basil leaves.
6. Serve caprese stuffed avocados immediately.
7. Enjoy!

4
servings

280

25 mins

Quinoa and Black Bean Salad

Ingredients:

- 1 cup quinoa (cooked and cooled)
- 1 can (15 oz) black beans (drained and rinsed)
- 1 cup corn kernels (fresh or frozen, cooked)
- 1 red bell pepper (diced)
- 1/4 cup red onion (finely chopped)
- 1/4 cup fresh cilantro leaves (chopped)
- Juice of 2 limes
- 2 tbsp extra virgin olive oil
- 1 tsp cumin
- Salt and black pepper to taste
- Avocado slices (for garnish, optional)
- Lime wedges (for garnish)

Fun Facts

Quinoa and black bean salad is a hearty and nutritious vegetarian dish that's full of flavor.

Enjoy a hearty and nutritious quinoa and black bean salad. Quinoa is tossed with black beans, corn, bell peppers, and a zesty lime dressing for a satisfying and protein-packed vegetarian voyage.

Directions

1. In a large bowl, combine cooked and cooled quinoa, drained and rinsed black beans, corn kernels, diced red bell pepper, and finely chopped red onion.
2. In a small bowl, whisk together lime juice, extra virgin olive oil, cumin, salt, and black pepper.
3. Pour the lime dressing over the quinoa and black bean mixture. Toss to combine.
4. Garnish with chopped fresh cilantro leaves and avocado slices if desired.
5. Serve quinoa and black bean salad with lime wedges.
6. Enjoy!

4
servings

250

20 mins

Zucchini Noodles with Pesto

Ingredients:

- 4 medium zucchinis (spiralized into noodles)
- 1 cup fresh basil leaves
- 1/2 cup grated Parmesan cheese
- 1/4 cup pine nuts
- 2 cloves garlic (minced)
- 1/2 cup extra virgin olive oil
- Juice of 1 lemon
- Salt and black pepper to taste
- Cherry tomatoes (for garnish)
- Grated Parmesan cheese (for garnish, optional)
- Fresh basil leaves (for garnish)
- Lemon wedges (for garnish)

Fun Facts

Zucchini noodles with pesto are a light and refreshing vegetarian dish that's perfect for summer.

Dive into a plate of zucchini noodles with pesto. Spiralized zucchini noodles are coated in a vibrant and herbaceous pesto sauce for a light and refreshing vegetarian voyage.

Directions

1. In a food processor, combine fresh basil leaves, grated Parmesan cheese, pine nuts, minced garlic, and lemon juice.
2. Pulse until ingredients are finely chopped.
3. With the food processor running, slowly drizzle in extra virgin olive oil until the pesto is smooth and well combined.
4. Season the pesto with salt and black pepper to taste. Adjust lemon juice or olive oil if desired.
5. In a large skillet, heat a drizzle of olive oil over medium heat.
6. Add spiralized zucchini noodles to the skillet and sauté for 2-3 mins until they are tender.
7. Toss the zucchini noodles with the prepared pesto sauce.
8. Garnish with cherry tomatoes, grated Parmesan cheese, fresh basil leaves, and lemon wedges if desired.
9. Serve zucchini noodles with pesto immediately.
10. Enjoy!

4
servings

360

45 mins

Eggplant Parmesan

Indulge in the classic Italian flavors of eggplant parmesan. Slices of eggplant are breaded, fried until golden, layered with marinara sauce and mozzarella cheese, then baked to perfection for a comforting vegetarian voyage.

Ingredients:

- 2 large eggplants (sliced into 1/2-inch rounds)
- 2 cups marinara sauce
- 2 cups shredded mozzarella cheese
- 1 cup grated Parmesan cheese
- 1 cup all-purpose flour
- 3 large eggs
- 2 cups breadcrumbs
- 2 tsp dried oregano
- Salt and black pepper to taste
- Fresh basil leaves (for garnish)
- Cooked spaghetti or pasta (for serving, optional)

Directions

1. Preheat oven to 375°F (190°C).
2. In a shallow dish, place all-purpose flour.
3. In another shallow dish, beat eggs.
4. In a third shallow dish, combine breadcrumbs, dried oregano, salt, and black pepper.
5. Dredge eggplant slices in flour, dip in beaten eggs, and coat with breadcrumb mixture, pressing gently to adhere.
6. Heat vegetable oil in a large skillet over medium-high heat.
7. Fry breaded eggplant slices for 2-3 mins per side until golden brown. Drain on paper towels.
8. In a baking dish, spread a thin layer of marinara sauce.
9. Arrange a layer of fried eggplant slices on top of the sauce.
10. Sprinkle with shredded mozzarella cheese and grated Parmesan cheese.
11. Repeat the layers until all ingredients are used, finishing with cheese on top.
12. Bake in the preheated oven for 25-30 mins, or until the cheese is melted and bubbly.
13. Garnish with fresh basil leaves.
14. Serve eggplant parmesan over cooked spaghetti or pasta if desired.
15. Enjoy!

Fun Facts

Eggplant parmesan is a comforting and classic Italian dish that's perfect for indulgence.

4
servings

290

50 mins

Stuffed Bell Peppers with Quinoa

Ingredients:

- 4 large bell peppers (any color)
- 1 cup quinoa (cooked)
- 1 can (15 oz) black beans (drained and rinsed)
- 1 cup corn kernels (fresh or frozen, cooked)
- 1 cup salsa (mild or hot, as per preference)
- 1 tsp chili powder
- 1/2 tsp ground cumin
- Salt and black pepper to taste
- Shredded cheddar cheese (for topping, optional)
- Fresh cilantro leaves (for garnish)
- Lime wedges (for garnish)

Fun Facts

Stuffed bell peppers with quinoa are a hearty and nutritious vegetarian dish.

Delight in the wholesome goodness of stuffed bell peppers with quinoa. Bell peppers are filled with a flavorful mixture of quinoa, black beans, corn, and spices, then baked to perfection for a hearty vegetarian voyage.

Directions

1. Preheat oven to 375°F (190°C).
2. Cut the tops off the bell peppers and remove the seeds and membranes.
3. In a large bowl, combine cooked quinoa, drained and rinsed black beans, cooked corn kernels, salsa, chili powder, ground cumin, salt, and black pepper. Mix well.
4. Stuff each bell pepper with the quinoa and black bean mixture.
5. Place stuffed bell peppers in a baking dish.
6. If desired, top each stuffed pepper with shredded cheddar cheese.
7. Cover the baking dish with aluminum foil and bake for 30-35 mins, or until the peppers are tender.
8. Remove the foil and bake for an additional 5 mins to melt the cheese if added.
9. Garnish with fresh cilantro leaves and serve with lime wedges.
10. Enjoy!

4
servings

380

45 mins

Creamy Tomato Basil Risotto

Dive into the creamy goodness of tomato basil risotto. Arborio rice is simmered in a luscious tomato and basil-infused broth, then finished with Parmesan cheese for a comforting and flavorful vegetarian voyage.

Ingredients:

- 1 1/2 cups Arborio rice
- 4 cups vegetable broth
- 1 can (14 oz) crushed tomatoes
- 1/2 cup fresh basil leaves (chopped)
- 1/2 cup grated Parmesan cheese
- 1 onion (finely chopped)
- 2 cloves garlic (minced)
- 2 tbsp extra virgin olive oil
- Salt and black pepper to taste
- Fresh basil leaves (for garnish)
- Grated Parmesan cheese (for garnish, optional)
- Cherry tomatoes (for garnish, optional)

Directions

1. In a saucepan, heat vegetable broth over low heat and keep it warm.
2. In a large skillet, heat extra virgin olive oil over medium heat.
3. Add finely chopped onion and minced garlic. Sauté for 2-3 mins until onion is translucent.
4. Add Arborio rice to the skillet and stir to coat with the olive oil, onion, and garlic.
5. Pour in crushed tomatoes and chopped fresh basil leaves. Stir to combine.
6. Begin adding warm vegetable broth to the rice mixture, one ladle at a time, stirring constantly and allowing the liquid to be absorbed before adding more.
7. Continue this process until the rice is creamy and cooked al dente, about 18-20 mins.
8. Stir in grated Parmesan cheese and season with salt and black pepper to taste.
9. Garnish with fresh basil leaves, grated Parmesan cheese, and cherry tomatoes if desired.
10. Serve creamy tomato basil risotto immediately.
11. Enjoy!

Fun Facts

Creamy tomato basil risotto is a comforting and flavorful vegetarian dish that's perfect for indulgence.

4 servings | **320** | **35 mins**

Chickpea and Spinach Curry

Ingredients:

- 2 cans (15 oz each) chickpeas (drained and rinsed)
- 1 can (14 oz) diced tomatoes
- 2 cups fresh spinach leaves
- 1 can (14 oz) coconut milk
- 1 onion (finely chopped)
- 3 cloves garlic (minced)
- 1-inch piece fresh ginger (minced)
- 2 tbsp curry powder
- 1 tsp ground cumin
- 1 tsp ground coriander
- 1/2 tsp ground turmeric
- 1/4 tsp cayenne pepper (adjust to taste)
- 2 tbsp vegetable oil
- Salt and black pepper to taste
- Fresh cilantro leaves (for garnish)
- Cooked rice (for serving)

Fun Facts

Chickpea and spinach curry is a fragrant and satisfying vegetarian dish with rich flavors.

Indulge in the aromatic and flavorful chickpea and spinach curry. Chickpeas are simmered in a rich and fragrant tomato-based sauce with spinach, spices, and coconut milk for a comforting vegetarian voyage.

Directions

1. In a large skillet, heat vegetable oil over medium heat.
2. Add finely chopped onion, minced garlic, and minced fresh ginger. Sauté for 2-3 mins until onion is translucent.
3. Add curry powder, ground cumin, ground coriander, ground turmeric, and cayenne pepper. Stir and cook for 1-2 mins until fragrant.
4. Pour in diced tomatoes and cook for 5 mins, breaking up the tomatoes with a spoon.
5. Add drained and rinsed chickpeas and coconut milk. Stir to combine.
6. Simmer the chickpea curry for 10-15 mins, allowing the flavors to meld together.
7. Stir in fresh spinach leaves and cook until wilted.
8. Season with salt and black pepper to taste.
9. Serve chickpea and spinach curry over cooked rice.
10. Garnish with fresh cilantro leaves.
11. Enjoy!

4 servings

240 kcal

25 mins

Cauliflower Fried Rice

Ingredients:

- 1 head cauliflower (grated or processed into rice-like texture)
- 1 cup frozen peas and carrots
- 1/2 cup corn kernels (fresh or frozen)
- 2 eggs (beaten)
- 3 cloves garlic (minced)
- 2 tbsp soy sauce
- 1 tbsp sesame oil
- 2 green onions (chopped)
- Salt and black pepper to taste
- Fresh cilantro leaves (for garnish)
- Lime wedges (for garnish)

Fun Facts

Cauliflower fried rice is a low-carb and healthy vegetarian dish that's packed with flavor.

Savor the savory goodness of cauliflower fried rice. Grated cauliflower is stir-fried with vegetables, eggs, and soy sauce for a low-carb and healthy vegetarian voyage that's packed with flavor.

Directions

1. Grate or process the cauliflower into rice-like texture using a food processor.
2. In a large skillet, heat a drizzle of vegetable oil over medium-high heat.
3. Add minced garlic and stir-fry for 1 min until fragrant.
4. Add frozen peas, carrots, and corn kernels. Stir-fry for 2-3 mins until vegetables are tender.
5. Push the vegetables to one side of the skillet and pour the beaten eggs into the empty side.
6. Scramble the eggs and mix them with the cooked vegetables.
7. Stir in grated cauliflower, soy sauce, and sesame oil. Cook for 5-7 mins, stirring occasionally, until cauliflower is tender.
8. Season with salt and black pepper to taste.
9. Garnish with chopped green onions, fresh cilantro leaves, and lime wedges if desired.
10. Serve cauliflower fried rice immediately.
11. Enjoy!

4 servings

350

50 mins

Sweet Potato and Chickpea Tagine

Indulge in the exotic flavors of sweet potato and chickpea tagine. Tender sweet potatoes and chickpeas are simmered in a fragrant and spiced tomato sauce with apricots, almonds, and couscous for a delightful vegetarian voyage.

Ingredients:

- 2 large sweet potatoes (peeled and diced)
- 2 cans (15 oz each) chickpeas (drained and rinsed)
- 1 can (14 oz) diced tomatoes
- 1/2 cup dried apricots (chopped)
- 1/4 cup slivered almonds
- 1 onion (finely chopped)
- 3 cloves garlic (minced)
- 2 tsp ground cumin
- 1 tsp ground cinnamon
- 1 tsp ground coriander
- 1/2 tsp ground turmeric
- 1/4 tsp cayenne pepper (adjust to taste)
- 2 cups vegetable broth
- 1 cup couscous
- 2 tbsp vegetable oil
- Salt and black pepper to taste
- Fresh cilantro leaves (for garnish)
- Lemon wedges (for garnish)

Directions

1. In a large skillet or tagine, heat vegetable oil over medium heat.
2. Add finely chopped onion and minced garlic. Sauté for 2-3 mins until onion is translucent.
3. Add ground cumin, ground cinnamon, ground coriander, ground turmeric, and cayenne pepper. Stir and cook for 1-2 mins until fragrant.
4. Add diced sweet potatoes, drained and rinsed chickpeas, diced tomatoes, chopped dried apricots, slivered almonds, and vegetable broth. Stir to combine.
5. Bring to a simmer and cover. Cook for 25-30 mins, or until sweet potatoes are tender.
6. In a separate pot, prepare couscous according to package instructions.
7. Fluff the couscous with a fork.
8. Season the sweet potato and chickpea tagine with salt and black pepper to taste.
9. Serve the tagine over cooked couscous.
10. Garnish with fresh cilantro leaves and lemon wedges if desired.
11. Enjoy!

Fun Facts

Sweet potato and chickpea tagine is a fragrant and exotic vegetarian dish that's full of flavor.

Chapter 11:
Sweet Endings

4 servings

240

15 mins

Chocolate Avocado Mousse

Ingredients:

- 2 ripe avocados (peeled and pitted)
- 1/4 cup cocoa powder
- 1/4 cup maple syrup or honey
- 1 tsp vanilla extract
- Pinch of salt
- Fresh berries (for garnish)
- Whipped cream (for garnish, optional)
- Chocolate shavings (for garnish, optional)

Indulge in the creamy and guilt-free indulgence of chocolate avocado mousse. Ripe avocados are blended with cocoa powder, sweetener, and vanilla extract for a luscious and healthy sweet ending.

Directions

1. In a food processor or blender, combine ripe avocados, cocoa powder, maple syrup or honey, vanilla extract, and a pinch of salt.
2. Blend until smooth and creamy, scraping down the sides of the bowl as needed.
3. Taste and adjust the sweetness if needed by adding more maple syrup or honey.
4. Divide the chocolate avocado mousse into serving glasses or bowls.
5. Chill in the refrigerator for at least 1 hour to set.
6. Garnish with fresh berries, whipped cream, and chocolate shavings if desired.
7. Enjoy!

Fun Facts

Chocolate avocado mousse is a creamy and healthy dessert that's perfect for chocolate lovers.

9 bars | 320 | 45 mins

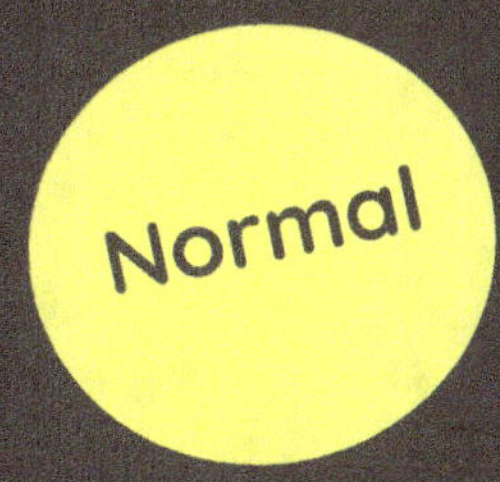

Raspberry Cheesecake Bars

Ingredients:

- 1 1/2 cups graham cracker crumbs
- 1/2 cup unsalted butter (melted)
- 2 cups cream cheese (room temperature)
- 1/2 cup granulated sugar
- 2 large eggs
- 1 tsp vanilla extract
- 1/2 cup raspberry puree (fresh or frozen raspberries blended and strained)
- Fresh raspberries (for garnish)
- Powdered sugar (for dusting, optional)

Fun Facts

Raspberry cheesecake bars are a decadent and fruity dessert perfect for any occasion.

Delight in the decadence of raspberry cheesecake bars. A buttery graham cracker crust is topped with a creamy cheesecake layer and swirls of raspberry puree for a fruity and luscious sweet ending.

Directions

1. Preheat oven to 325°F (160°C).
2. In a bowl, combine graham cracker crumbs and melted unsalted butter. Mix until the crumbs are evenly coated.
3. Press the graham cracker mixture into the bottom of a greased 9x9-inch (23x23 cm) baking pan.
4. In a separate bowl, beat cream cheese and granulated sugar until smooth.
5. Add eggs and vanilla extract. Continue to beat until well combined.
6. Pour the cream cheese mixture over the graham cracker crust.
7. Dollop raspberry puree over the cream cheese mixture.
8. Use a knife or toothpick to swirl the raspberry puree into the cream cheese mixture to create a marbled effect.
9. Bake in the preheated oven for 35-40 mins, or until the cheesecake is set and the edges are lightly golden.
10. Remove from the oven and let it cool to room temperature.
11. Refrigerate for at least 2 hours to chill and set completely.
12. Cut into bars, garnish with fresh raspberries, and dust with powdered sugar if desired.
13. Enjoy!

12
cookies

120

20 mins

3-Ingredient Peanut Butter Cookies

Ingredients:

- 1 cup peanut butter (creamy or crunchy)
- 1 cup granulated sugar
- 1 large egg
- Coarse sea salt (for sprinkling, optional)

Satisfy your sweet tooth with 3-ingredient peanut butter cookies. These easy and flourless cookies are made with peanut butter, sugar, and an egg for a quick and delicious sweet ending.

Directions

1. Preheat oven to 350°F (175°C).
2. In a bowl, combine peanut butter, granulated sugar, and a large egg.
3. Mix until all ingredients are well combined.
4. Scoop tablespoon-sized portions of the cookie dough and place them on a baking sheet lined with parchment paper.
5. Use a fork to flatten each cookie and create a crisscross pattern on top.
6. If desired, sprinkle coarse sea salt on top of each cookie for a sweet and salty touch.
7. Bake in the preheated oven for 10-12 mins, or until the edges are lightly golden.
8. Remove from the oven and let the cookies cool on the baking sheet for a few minutes before transferring them to a wire rack to cool completely.
9. Enjoy!

Fun Facts

3-ingredient peanut butter cookies are a quick and easy treat for peanut butter lovers.

6
servings

160

30 mins

Lemon Sorbet
with Fresh Berries

Refresh your palate with lemon sorbet with fresh berries. This homemade sorbet is bursting with zesty lemon flavor and served with a medley of fresh berries for a refreshing and tangy sweet ending.

Ingredients:

- 1 1/2 cups fresh lemon juice (from about 6-8 lemons)
- 1 1/2 cups water
- 1 1/4 cups granulated sugar
- Zest of 1 lemon
- Fresh mixed berries (strawberries, blueberries, raspberries, blackberries, for serving)
- Fresh mint leaves (for garnish)
- Lemon slices (for garnish, optional)
- Powdered sugar (for dusting, optional)

Directions

1. In a saucepan, combine water and granulated sugar. Heat over medium heat, stirring, until the sugar is dissolved.
2. Remove from heat and let the sugar syrup cool to room temperature.
3. Stir in fresh lemon juice and lemon zest.
4. Pour the lemon mixture into an ice cream maker and churn according to the manufacturer's instructions until it reaches a sorbet consistency.
5. Transfer the lemon sorbet to a lidded container and freeze for at least 4 hours or until firm.
6. Before serving, let the sorbet sit at room temperature for a few minutes to soften slightly for easier scooping.
7. Serve lemon sorbet in bowls or glasses, garnished with fresh mixed berries, mint leaves, lemon slices, and a dusting of powdered sugar if desired.
8. Enjoy the refreshing tanginess!

Fun Facts

Lemon sorbet with fresh berries is a light and tangy dessert perfect for summer.

12 servings

180

20 mins

Nutella-Stuffed Strawberries

Ingredients:

- 12 fresh strawberries (washed and dried)
- Nutella hazelnut spread (or chocolate hazelnut spread of choice)
- Powdered sugar (for dusting, optional)
- Chopped hazelnuts (for garnish, optional)

Fun Facts

Nutella-stuffed strawberries are a simple and indulgent dessert for Nutella lovers.

Indulge in the delightful combination of Nutella-stuffed strawberries. Fresh strawberries are filled with creamy Nutella hazelnut spread for a sweet and satisfying sweet ending.

Directions

1. Using a small paring knife, carefully cut off the tops of the strawberries to create a flat base.
2. Hollow out the center of each strawberry using a small spoon or strawberry huller to create a cavity for the filling.
3. Fill each strawberry with a generous amount of Nutella hazelnut spread.
4. If desired, sprinkle powdered sugar over the filled strawberries for added sweetness.
5. Garnish with chopped hazelnuts if desired.
6. Arrange Nutella-stuffed strawberries on a serving platter.
7. Enjoy these sweet and creamy delights!

18 macaroons

100

30 mins

Coconut Macaroons

Ingredients:

- 3 cups shredded sweetened coconut
- 2/3 cup sweetened condensed milk
- 1 tsp vanilla extract
- Pinch of salt
- Egg whites from 2 large eggs
- Maraschino cherries (for topping, optional)

Fun Facts

Coconut macaroons are a classic and gluten-free sweet treat for coconut enthusiasts.

Delight in the sweet and chewy goodness of coconut macaroons. These gluten-free treats are made with shredded coconut, sweetened condensed milk, and a hint of vanilla extract for a classic sweet ending.

Directions

1. Preheat oven to 325°F (160°C).
2. In a bowl, combine shredded sweetened coconut, sweetened condensed milk, vanilla extract, and a pinch of salt. Mix until well combined.
3. In a separate bowl, beat the egg whites until stiff peaks form.
4. Gently fold the beaten egg whites into the coconut mixture until fully incorporated.
5. Use a cookie scoop or your hands to shape the coconut mixture into small mounds and place them on a baking sheet lined with parchment paper.
6. If desired, top each macaroon with a maraschino cherry.
7. Bake in the preheated oven for 18-20 mins, or until the macaroons are lightly golden on the outside and still slightly soft in the center.
8. Remove from the oven and let the macaroons cool on the baking sheet for a few minutes before transferring them to a wire rack to cool completely.
9. Enjoy the sweet and chewy coconut macaroons!

6 servings

280

20 mins

Caramel Apple Slices

Ingredients:

- 3 apples (sliced into wedges)
- 1/2 cup caramel sauce (store-bought or homemade)
- Chopped nuts (such as peanuts or pecans, for topping)
- Mini chocolate chips (for topping, optional)
- Sprinkles (for topping, optional)
- Whipped cream (for topping, optional)

Fun Facts

Caramel apple slices are a delightful and customizable dessert for apple lovers.

Enjoy the perfect blend of sweet and tart with caramel apple slices. Crisp apple slices are drizzled with warm caramel sauce and topped with your favorite nuts or toppings for a delightful sweet ending.

Directions

1. Slice the apples into wedges, removing the core and seeds.
2. Arrange the apple slices on a serving platter or individual plates.
3. Warm the caramel sauce in the microwave or on the stovetop until it's pourable but not too hot.
4. Drizzle the warm caramel sauce over the apple slices.
5. Sprinkle chopped nuts, mini chocolate chips, sprinkles, or whipped cream on top of the caramel-covered apples, as desired.
6. Enjoy the sweet and crunchy goodness of caramel apple slices!

4
servings

220

10 mins

Banana Chocolate Chip Ice Cream

Ingredients:

- 4 ripe bananas (peeled, sliced, and frozen)
- 1/2 cup chocolate chips (semi-sweet or dark)
- 1 tsp vanilla extract
- Chopped nuts (for topping, optional)
- Chocolate sauce (for drizzling, optional)
- Whipped cream (for topping, optional)
- Maraschino cherries (for garnish, optional)

Fun Facts

Banana chocolate chip ice cream is a simple and healthy dessert perfect for banana lovers.

Cool down with homemade banana chocolate chip ice cream. Frozen bananas are blended with chocolate chips and a touch of vanilla extract for a creamy and guilt-free sweet ending.

Directions

1. Place the frozen banana slices in a food processor or blender.
2. Add chocolate chips and vanilla extract.
3. Blend until the mixture becomes smooth and creamy, scraping down the sides of the bowl as needed.
4. If the ice cream is too soft, you can transfer it to a lidded container and freeze for an additional 30 mins to firm up.
5. Scoop banana chocolate chip ice cream into bowls or cones.
6. Top with chopped nuts, chocolate sauce, whipped cream, and a maraschino cherry if desired.
7. Enjoy the creamy and guilt-free treat!

18
truffles

140

40 mins

Mint Chocolate Truffles

Ingredients:

- 8 oz dark chocolate (chopped)
- 1/2 cup heavy cream
- 1/4 tsp mint extract
- Green food coloring (optional)
- Cocoa powder (for dusting)
- Crushed peppermint candies (for garnish, optional)
- White chocolate (for drizzling, optional)

Fun Facts

Mint chocolate truffles are a decadent and refreshing dessert for chocolate lovers.

Indulge in the rich and creamy mint chocolate truffles. These bite-sized delights are made with dark chocolate, heavy cream, and a hint of mint extract, then coated in more chocolate for a decadent sweet ending.

Directions

1. In a microwave-safe bowl, heat the heavy cream until it begins to boil.
2. Place the chopped dark chocolate in a separate bowl.
3. Pour the hot cream over the chocolate and let it sit for 1-2 mins.
4. Stir the chocolate and cream mixture until smooth and well combined.
5. If desired, add mint extract and a few drops of green food coloring to the mixture. Stir until fully incorporated.
6. Cover the mixture and refrigerate for about 2 hours, or until it's firm enough to handle.
7. Once the mixture is firm, use a spoon or a melon baller to scoop out portions and roll them into small truffle-sized balls.
8. Place the truffles on a parchment-lined tray and refrigerate for another 15-20 mins to firm up.
9. If desired, dust the truffles with cocoa powder or garnish with crushed peppermint candies.
10. For an extra touch, you can drizzle melted white chocolate over the truffles.
11. Chill the truffles in the refrigerator until they're set.
12. Enjoy the rich and creamy mint chocolate truffles!

24 bites   130   30 mins

Pecan Pie Bites

Ingredients:

- 1 1/4 cups all-purpose flour
- 1/4 tsp salt
- 1/2 cup unsalted butter (cold and cubed)
- 2-3 tbsp ice water
- 1 cup pecan halves
- 1/2 cup brown sugar (packed)
- 1/2 cup light corn syrup
- 2 large eggs
- 1 tsp vanilla extract
- Pinch of salt
- Whipped cream (for topping, optional)

Fun Facts

Pecan pie bites are a miniature and delicious version of the classic pecan pie.

Experience the flavors of pecan pie in bite-sized form with pecan pie bites. These mini treats feature a buttery pie crust filled with a sweet and nutty pecan filling for a delectable sweet ending.

Directions

1. In a food processor, combine all-purpose flour and salt.
2. Add cold, cubed unsalted butter and pulse until the mixture resembles coarse crumbs.
3. Gradually add ice water, 1 tablespoon at a time, and pulse until the dough comes together.
4. Shape the dough into a disk, wrap it in plastic wrap, and refrigerate for at least 30 mins.
5. Preheat oven to 350°F (175°C).
6. Roll out the chilled dough on a lightly floured surface to about 1/8-inch thickness.
7. Use a round cookie cutter or a small glass to cut out circles from the dough.
8. Press each dough circle into the cups of a mini muffin tin.
9. In a bowl, combine pecan halves, brown sugar, light corn syrup, eggs, vanilla extract, and a pinch of salt. Mix well.
10. Spoon the pecan filling into each mini pie crust.
11. Bake in the preheated oven for 20-25 mins, or until the pecan filling is set and the crust is golden brown.
12. Remove the pecan pie bites from the muffin tin and let them cool on a wire rack.
13. If desired, top with whipped cream before serving.
14. Enjoy the sweet and nutty goodness of pecan pie bites!

We have a small favor to ask

Dear Culinary Enthusiasts,

Our journey through the world of cooking, with "Weeknight Wonders: A 5-Ingredient Cookbook," has been nothing short of extraordinary. We hope you've found inspiration, convenience, and culinary delight in these pages, which are designed to make weeknight cooking a breeze and bring your family around the dinner table with smiles and satisfaction.

Creating this cookbook has been a labor of love, a tribute to the joy of preparing meals that are not only delicious but also easy to make after a long day's work. We've poured our passion for food and family into these recipes and are delighted to have you as part of our culinary community.

Now, we kindly request a small favor from you, our fellow food explorers. Reviews are the lifeblood of small, independent publishers like us. They serve as a compass for those who are on a quest for quick, delectable, and hassle-free meals to enjoy with their loved ones. Your review is a testament to the value of these recipes.

We invite you to share your thoughts and experiences by leaving a review, a simple star rating, and a brief sentence or two about your journey with "Weeknight Wonders." This gesture, on the platform or app where you acquired this cookbook, is invaluable to us. It not only helps us reach more cooking enthusiasts but also ensures that families worldwide can savor these uncomplicated culinary treasures.

As the creators of this cookbook, we treasure and consider every review with care and gratitude. Your insights, whether they express satisfaction or offer constructive feedback, are invaluable. They are the driving force behind our commitment to continually provide you with the most straightforward, delicious, and family-friendly recipes.

While our aim is to present you with perfect, foolproof recipes, we understand that the path to culinary excellence is not without the occasional hiccup. Your reviews serve as our guiding light, pointing out areas where we can improve, innovate, and enhance your cooking experience.

In closing, we want to express our profound gratitude for selecting "Weeknight Wonders: A 5-Ingredient Cookbook" as your culinary companion. Your choice, trust, and active participation in this culinary journey are a constant source of inspiration.

As we look forward to many more weeknight dinners filled with joy, deliciousness, and togetherness, we wholeheartedly thank you for being part of our culinary family. Your experience matters, your voice matters, and we can't wait to explore more culinary wonders with you.

With heartfelt appreciation and a passion for family meals,